COLLINS GEM GUIDES

illustrated by
Bruce Pearson

text by
John A. Burton

COLLINS
London and Glasgow

Acknowledgements

Especial thanks are due to Vivien G. Burton for typing all the various drafts and preparing the index, to Bill Griffith for reading the final text and to Howard Loxton of William Collins for guiding it through to publication.

The names used in this book follow *A World List of Mammalian Species* by G.B. Corbet and J.E. Hill (British Museum, Natural History and Cornell University, 1980).

First published 1984

© in the text John A. Burton 1984
© in the illustrations Bruce Pearson 1984

ISBN 0 00 458814 2

Colour reproduction by Adroit Photo-Litho Ltd, Birmingham

Filmset by Servis Filmsetting Ltd, Manchester

Printed and bound by Wm Collins Sons and Co Ltd, Glasgow

Reprint 10 9 8 7 6 5 4 3 2 1

Contents

About this book

The purpose of this book is to provide information on the mammals most likely to be seen on a visit to a zoo, where most of us see 'wild' animals, for few people are lucky enough to see more than a tiny fraction of the world's animals in their natural habitat.

The animals are arranged in their Orders (main groupings, see p. 3). Detailed descriptions are not given when the illustration fulfils this purpose. Information on habitat, life cycle, feeding, behaviour, etc is, whenever possible, based on animals in the wild but in many cases the breeding biology in particular has only been studied in captivity. The best zoos increasingly emphasize the conservation of rare and endangered species and wherever possible the text draws attention to the role which zoos are playing in building up captive stocks.

Animals are described by their Common and their Scientific names which consist of 2 latin words: the Genus (which is capitalised) and the species name. Thus the Indian Elephant is *Elephas maximas*. A third name is used for a subspecies. When repeated, the Genus may be abbreviated to its first letter. Scientific names are occasionally altered by zoologists in order to show relationships with other species. Consequently the names used in a modern book may differ from those in older ones. Unfortunately some zoo labels are out-of-date and names used may differ from those used here.

Introduction

Some of the earliest records of civilization refer to menageries and collections of sacred animals which were the forerunners of modern zoos. When Cortez led his conquistadors into the Aztec capital, where Mexico City now stands, he found a large zoo with bison, jaguar and hundreds of other animals, and most medieval European rulers had menageries of

FEEDING TIMES

PENGUINS   1.15

SEA LIONS   2.00

some sort. Britain's was housed in the Tower of London. According to legend, when the last of the ravens disappears the Tower will fall; consequently, although the rest of the Royal Menagerie was transferred to London Zoo, the ravens are still kept.

The modern zoo has two distinct origins: first the travelling menagerie, which visited fairs and circuses – rather squalid sideshows of which some still exist; second the nineteenth-century thirst for knowledge which, combined with British colonisation and wealth, led to the formation of the Zoological Society of London and the opening of the Zoological Gardens – the first 'Zoo' – in 1828. Within a year it had attracted nearly 250,000 visitors. This was a scientific establishment, and although today we may frown upon many of the practices and attitudes of those times, it was to set a standard and led directly to the founding of other eminent zoos.

Throughout their history serious zoos have had to compete with purely commercial establishments, which aim only to make as much money as possible for their owners. Such zoos concentrate upon the spectacular: lions, tigers, bears, monkeys and a few large antelope, zebra and ostrich, and usually ignore the smaller, less spectacular animals. In the 1960s there was a vogue for dolphinaria and they sprang up all over the world, making a fast buck for their owners, and then with a rise in public interest in conservation of whales and dolphins, they nearly all disappeared. Fortunately there are still some excellent dolphinaria where the training of dolphins to

perform is an integral part of scientific research into their communication systems.

Do not visit bad zoos, your money would help them to survive. A modern, progressive zoo will have a concern for the welfare of its animals and be active in the fields of scientific research, public education and wildlife conservation. Sadly, only a few of the world's zoos can claim to be active in all three fields but more and more are striving in this direction.

Food

Some zoos now exhibit food preparation rooms complete with keepers preparing animal rations, and almost all the better zoos ban feeding by the public. A modern zoo feeds carefully calculated, balanced diets complete with vitamins and mineral additives. In a few of the really good zoos animals will also be given food which provides 'occupational therapy' – such as giving monkeys twigs and shoots which they can pull apart, rather than just highly nutritious, but boring, pellets.

Health and hygiene

A good zoo will have its animals in tip-top condition and the cages kept scrupulously clean. In the early zoos tropical animals were often kept in suffocating heat, until it was found that, provided they had a warm, dry and draught-free lair to retreat to, most animals were much healthier if they were given access to plenty of fresh air. A modern zoo cage will often be tiled with curved corners for easy cleaning, but to compensate for its sterility the inhabitants should be given climbing frames, sterilized litter to dig in, branches to break up, nest building materials and interesting food. Some of the most interesting exhibits, where the animals are behaving most naturally, are totally artificial environments.

The vet is an important member of the staff of any zoo. A good way of finding out how good a zoo is would be to ask if they have a vet on the staff or as a

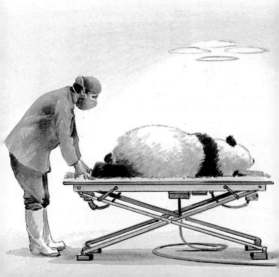

regular visitor. His (or her) patients cannot describe their symptoms and many of the animals kept in zoos are relatively unknown, so diagnosing illness, or even noticing that an animal is out of condition would be very difficult if good keepers were not usually aware when one of their charges is not fit.

Education

The education of visitors was the main reason for establishing the first Zoological Garden in London, and even today it should be the most important function of a zoo. Despite television and increased travel, the only place most people get a chance to see live wild animals at close quarters is in a zoo. The modern zoo should have as much information as possible on the exhibit labels, but regretably few do.

A good label, in addition to the name of the species, will have information on its distribution (such as a map), together with a note on its status, as well as pointing out anything interesting about its biology, ecology and behaviour. Some zoos employ professional lecturers and guides to take parties of visitors around the collection, explaining about the animals as they go. Another form of guided tour is provided with tape-cassettes or talking 'labels'. Scattered throughout a modern zoo are often special exhibitions detailing scientific aspects of the zoo's work – ecology, conservation or a similar topic. An important part of a zoo's education service is often a membership section with regular lectures, behind-the-scenes tours, open nights, newsletters and other activities. A zoo which has a friends or supporters or members section to back it up will generally be one of the more outward going, with higher standards.

Conservation

Zoos have come to be described as the new Arks: places where endangered species can be saved. Sadly, there are far too many species endangered for zoos ever to be able to save more than a tiny handful. The main cause of animals becoming rare is undoubtedly habitat destruction, particularly in the tropics where the rainforests are being destroyed at an alarming rate. In addition to this, many animals are hunted and trapped: elephants killed for their ivory, rhinos for their horn, ocelots for their skins, musk deer for their

scent glands, whales for their blubber etc. In the recent past another threat was capture for the zoo trade, but in recent years many zoos have started breeding a large proportion of the animals they exhibit, including many of the rarities. A few zoos, such as Jersey Wildlife Preservation Trust, specialise in breeding endangered species, with the objective of releasing them back into the wild. Many others also put a lot of their resources into breeding endangered species and a few, notably Frankfurt and New York, spend large sums of money on conservation in the field as well. Many zoos give space to exhibitions by conservation organisations such as the World

Wildlife Fund and, since 1974, The Fauna and Flora Preservation Society has been organising a conference every few years, in cooperation with the world's leading zoos, to discuss the role of zoos and captive breeding in conservation programmes.

Zoo breeding

Although a single zoo can sometimes keep enough of an animal to breed them for a few years, generally it is necessary to interbreed with other populations, to prevent them becoming inbred. In recent years the world's leading zoos have been cooperating more and

more. Competition between zoos to have the 'rarest' or the 'most valuable' has gone, since zoos avoid putting a value on a rare species and never sell them, but only lend or exchange them. Unfortunately there are still unscrupulous dealers and, as I write, a Belgian dealer has recently smuggled from Brazil nearly 30 Golden-head Lion Tamarins – which may be one third of the total surviving in the world. Immediately the international zoo world put an embargo on these animals and in such circumstances insist that they are returned to their country of origin. If this is impossible then they should be deposited with a reputable zoo for breeding and eventual return to the wild.

One of the most famous examples of cooperation resulted when the Fauna Preservation Society (now 'and Flora') organized the expedition which captured 3 of the last wild Arabian Oryx (see p. 354) and established the World Herd of Oryx, together with London Zoo and several American Zoos. As a result of two decades of cooperation not only were the Arabian Oryx bred in sufficient numbers to be sent back to Jordan and Oman, but they were also dispersed to other zoos so that separate herds could be started up.

Breeding successes and failures

Some animals are now being bred in such numbers that zoos no longer need to import them from the wild, but the real achievement is when they can be bred through several generations to become self-sustaining in captivity. With some species such success seems elusive. The Giant Panda is among the most popular of zoo animals but, despite some of the most sophisticated research and careful husbandry ever given to a single species, only a handful have been bred in captivity. Although there are more and more gorillas and orang utans bred in captivity each year only a few have been born to parents which were themselves born in captivity. It seems unlikely that either of these species will be self-sustaining in captivity before the end of the century.

Reintroduction into the wild

A breeding programme for conservation purposes usually aims to reintroduce the species to the wild. For such a programme to succeed enough suitable habitat must exist, and the reasons for the animal's original extinction must have been eliminated. Hence, although zoos are breeding a large surplus population of Siberian tigers each year (there are probably more in captivity than in the wild) there is no real hope of reintroduction because the areas into which they could be released already have tigers and it is doubtful that more could survive there. Tigers in captivity may well cause a dilemma in the future since dozens are bred each year and already zoos are sterilizing their animals; some zoos have sold their surplus to circuses and less scrupulous ones might start killing them to sell the skins for rugs.

For some species reintroduction has been feasible. One of the first successes was the European Bison (p. 338), saved largely by the efforts of Jan Sztoleman, a Polish zoologist who started the International Society for the Protection of the Bison. Zoos contributed pure-bred bison, which eventually formed the herd reintroduced into the Bialowieza Forest in Poland, and they have subsequently been released in reserves in Russia and Romania. The Lynx, although still relatively abundant in many parts of North America, Siberia and Russia, has disappeared from most of western Europe and, in recent years, Riber Castle Zoo in Britain has specialized in breeding Lynx, of several subspecies, for eventual reintroduction. The first have been released in France, but it will be 10 years or more before its success can be evaluated. The Arabian Oryx has already been mentioned. Like many other hoofed animals, Oryx are not only relatively easy to breed in captivity but also very suitable for reintroduction. Several species have been introduced into New Zealand and Texas, where they have proliferated. The European Beaver was exterminated over most of its range in western Europe, including Britain, several centuries ago and in recent years there have been 2 areas of introduction: one good, the other bad. In Scandinavia Cana-

European Bison

European Lynx

dian Beavers have been released, and there will almost certainly be an adverse effect upon the native European Beaver (at the very least they will interbreed, thereby losing pure-bred European Beavers). In France, Switzerland and Germany a successful programme has been undertaken to release European Beavers in some of their old haunts. Finally, in Britain European Otters have been bred in captivity and are now being released into areas where they had been exterminated.

Arabian Oryx

Beaver

ECHIDNA

The Short-nosed Echidna or Spiny Anteater *Tachyglossus aculeatus* grows to nearly 60 cm long and weighs up to 6 kg; it does not have a tail or external ears. It is found in Australia, Tasmania and south-eastern New Guinea, in a wide variety of habitats including open steppe country, woodland and forest. It feeds mainly on insects, particularly ants and termites, which it catches with its long anteater-like tongue. Since it lacks teeth, sand and grit

Short-nosed Echidna

are used to help grind up the food. It is one of the most primitive of mammals, sharing many characteristics with reptiles, such as its ability to go for periods of up to a month without feeding. It is an egg-laying mammal (Monotreme) and lays a single egg (occasionally 2 or 3) into a pouch rather like that of marsupials; after an incubation of 12 or more days it hatches and is suckled on milk secreted directly into the pouch, since there are no nipples. Once the spines begin to develop the female scratches the young out of the pouch and leaves them in a simple nest while she forages. The male possesses poison glands connected to a spur on the hind feet, but the echidna's normal defence is to dig itself rapidly into the ground, leaving only its spines protruding. Short-nosed Echidnas are seen in many zoos and have lived for over 15 years.

The much rarer Long-beaked Echidna *Zaglossus bruijni*, from New Guinea, is only occasionally seen in zoos. It is larger than the Short-nosed Echidna, weighing up to about 15 kg. Neither species normally breeds in zoos but the Long-beaked has lived for 30 years.

The only other species of egg-laying mammal is the Platypus *Ornithorhynchus anatinus* of the freshwaters of Australia and Tasmania, but this has only very rarely been seen in zoos outside Australia.

BRUSH-TAILED POSSUM
Trichosurus vulpecula

There are 3 closely related species of Brush-tailed Possums native to Australia. The Brush-tailed Possum is the species most commonly seen in zoos and is found wherever there is suitable habitat throughout Australia, as well as Tasmania and Kangaroo Island, but is absent from some of the more northern areas. It has been introduced into New Zealand, where it has become an extremely abundant pest. It is found in dry forests and woodlands, and also in treeless areas, living among rock clefts and in the burrows of other animals. A good climber (the tail is prehensile) and usually nocturnal, it hides in hollow trees, rock clefts and burrows by day. It grows to about 43 cm plus a tail of about 26 cm, and weighs just over 2 kg. Brush-tailed Possums feed on leaves and shoots, fruits of native trees and shrubs, and also take scraps of human food in suburban areas. They are a very adaptable species and are quite common in gardens and parks – and a frequent road casualty in many areas. Usually a single young (occasionally twins or triplets) is born after a gestation of up to 17 days; like all other marsupials they are helpless at birth and they first emerge from the pouch at 6–7 months. They are weaned between 8 and 11 months and become sexually mature after 2 years. Brush-tailed Possums are known to have lived over 13 years in the wild, and nearly 15 years in captivity. Often considered a pest because it damages garden plants and fruit trees, this possum is also an important fur-bearing animal. In a single year New Zealand's exports of possum furs have been as high as 1,605,000.

SUGAR GLIDER *Petaurus breviceps*

The Sugar Glider or Flying Phalanger is the marsupial equivalent of a flying squirrel, growing to a total length of about 36 cm of which the bushy tail is over half. Like flying squirrels it is not actually capable of true flight but makes extended leaps of up to 50 m by means of the gliding membrane which stretches along the flanks between the fore and hind feet. Sugar Gliders are widely distributed around the northern, eastern and southern sides of Australia and have been introduced into Tasmania; they occur in dry forests and woodlands. They live in small groups and are almost entirely arboreal, nesting in hollows in trees and rarely descending to the ground. They feed at night on nectar, blossoms, buds and insects. Two young are born into the mother's pouch, but soon emerge and cling to the mother's fur. Like some other marsupials the structure of their hind feet is unusual, the first toe lacks a claw and is opposable — giving the glider a 'thumb'. Sugar Gliders are the only species of glider likely to be seen in zoos outside Australia. They breed quite freely in captivity and are often very active.

The Squirrel Glider *P. norfolkensis* is closely related to the Sugar Glider, but larger with a more distinct stripe on its back; it is found in eastern Australia.

PADEMELONS

The 4 species of Pademelons or Scrub Wallabies are closely related to the Wallabies and Kangaroos (Macropus), and are similar in appearance. They are found in Australia, Tasmania, New Guinea and the Bismark Archipelago. The Red-bellied Pademelon *Thylogale billardieri* is also known as the Tasmanian Wallaby although it in fact formerly occurred in south-eastern South Australia and Victoria; although now extinct on the mainland it is often so common on Tasmania as to be considered a pest, and large numbers have been killed for their skins. The Dusky Pademelon *T. bruijni* is confined to eastern parts of New Guinea and the islands of the Bismarks,

Red-necked Pademelon

where they live in forests up to an altitude of 4200 m (13,650 ft). The Red-necked Pademelon *T. thetis* is found in the eastern parts of Queensland and New South Wales, and the Red-legged Pademelon *T. stigmatica* in forests of south-eastern New Guinea and eastern Australia. All the pademelons are mostly nocturnal, hiding in dense undergrowth during the daytime. They all produce a single young (occasionally twins) a year, after a gestation of about one month. The young spend about 25 weeks in the mother's pouch and are weaned about 4 months later. A Red-bellied Pademelon has lived for nearly 9 years in captivity and all have been bred in captivity.

The Quokka or Short-tailed Pademelon *Setonix brachyurus* is a rare rat-like species, found in a few coastal regions of south-western Australia; it is occasionally seen in zoos.

The Parma or White-throated Wallaby *Macropus parma*, which is approximately the same size (60 cm long, plus a tail of 40 cm) and similar in general appearance, was thought by 1932 to be extinct. It originally occurred in New South Wales, and was subsequently found on the island of Kawau off New Zealand where it had been introduced; animals from here were spread among zoos, where it thrives. In 1967 it was rediscovered in its native haunts. The Dama Wallaby or Tammar, *Macropus eugenii* was also rediscovered on Kawau island, and is similarly thriving in zoos; it never actually became extinct on the mainland, but only really thrives on Kangaroo Island, and a few other islands.

RED-NECKED WALLABY *Macropus rufogriseus*

The Red-necked or Bennett's Wallaby is found in Australia from south-western Queensland, southwards through to southern Victoria, Tasmania and Flinders' Island. It is found mostly in dry, open forest habitats. It has been introduced into England and also on the South Island of New Zealand. The Red-necked Wallaby grows to a length of about 100 cm, plus a tail of up to 70 cm. Over most of its range it is common in dry forest, open heath and in the coastal lands. The single young, in common with other wallabies and

kangaroos, is tiny and almost completely helpless when it is born, after a gestation of about 30 days. It remains in the pouch for several weeks, firmly attached to its mother's nipple.

Red-necked Wallabies are hardy and have adapted well to European climates. They breed freely in several zoos, most notably at Whipsnade, where several hundred live in large paddocks on exposed downland. They have been introduced into the Peak district of England and Ashdown Forest, where they have survived for over 30 years. It is estimated that at one time the New Zealand populations numbered some 750,000 but as a result of an extensive campaign to reduce their numbers, they were down to about 3500 by the 1960s. The race introduced into Britain derived from Tasmania, and is the type usually referred to as Bennett's Wallaby. In captivity they have lived for over 18 years. Most other wallabies are rarely seen in zoos outside Australia, and one species, the Toolache Wallaby *Macropus greyi* became extinct in the 1920s. The Toolache Wallaby was a large slender species with a dozen stripes on its posterior; it was apparently still relatively abundant at the turn of the present century but was hunted not only for its fur – bounties were also paid and it was exterminated because it competed with domestic livestock. It was closely related and rather similar to the Black-gloved Wallaby *M. irma*, and like that species was an extremely active agile wallaby that was considered good 'sport' by its killers.

GREY KANGAROOS

There are two closely related species of Grey Kangaroos, or Foresters: the Eastern Grey Kangaroo *Macropus giganteus* and the Western Grey (or Sooty or Black-faced) Kangaroo *M. fuliginosus*. The Western is found in open woodland in southern and southwestern Australia, while the eastern is found in similar habitats in eastern Australia and Tasmania. Grey kangaroos are among the largest marsupials, with a body of 140 cm and tail of 90 cm and a weight of up to 90 kg. They live in small parties, grazing on grasses and herbs and other vegetation, usually at

Eastern Grey Kangaroo

twilight or at night. The single young (or joey) weighs about 28 g at birth and is finally weaned at about 14 months. It overlaps with the next young in the pouch for shortly after a joey is born another is conceived, though its development after birth is delayed until the previous joey has left the pouch. The huge hind feet enable kangaroos to make enormous leaps, and males also fight with them. Like the Red Kangaroo, the Grey is persecuted by farmers and is also exploited for its meat and hide. The Eastern Grey Kangaroo is exhibited in many zoos where it breeds quite regularly and may live for 15 years or more. The Western Grey Kangaroo is rarely seen. When moving slowly they have a 'five-footed' gait, balancing on their tails and forelegs, while swinging the hind legs forward.

RED KANGAROO *Macropus rufus*

The Red or Plains Kangaroo is found over much of Australia's interior, mainly in open grass and scrub. It is the largest living marsupial with a head and body length of 1.5 m and a tail of 1 m; an old male may weigh up to 90 kg. Females are smoky-blue and often known as 'blue-fliers'. The reddish males are known as 'boomers'. When jumping, Red Kangaroos can reach speeds of 50 kmph (30 mph) and clear over 7.5 m with each leap, and heights of over 3 m. They are gregarious, living in bands as large as 100 animals, grazing on herbs and grasses. The single young (joey) is born at any time of the year after a gestation of about 33 days; however, the development of the

embryo can be delayed after mating. The joey stays in its mother's pouch for about 6 months. As it grows it leaves the pouch, but returns for safety. Most adult females in the wild with a young joey in the pouch are also accompanied by a well developed juvenile and have a fertile embryo awaiting development. Red Kangaroos have been extensively hunted for the meat and skin trade and also because they compete for sheep and cattle grazing. In many parts of their former range they have declined, but they are still locally abundant. It has been estimated that there are over 2 million Red Kangaroos in the plains of New South Wales. Red Kangaroos breed freely in many larger zoos, and have been bred through several generations. They may live 15 or more years in captivity.

TREE KANGAROOS

Bennett's Tree Kangaroo *D. bennettianus*

There are about 7 species of tree kangaroo – although some of the species may prove to have been described twice, since they are rather variable and occur over quite a large area. They occur mainly in mountainous rain forests in New Guinea and northeastern Queensland, Australia. Most species are occasionally seen in zoos, but among the most frequently seen are the Ornate or Goodfellow's Tree Kangaroo *Dendrolagus goodfellowi*, the Grizzled Tree Kangaroo *D. inustus* and Matschie's Tree Kangaroo, *D. matshiei*. Tree kangaroos are fairly large animals ranging in size between 52 cm and 80 cm long, plus a tail of up to 93 cm, and weighing up to about 9 kg. Some are rather strikingly marked and Matschei's Tree Kangaroo is one of the most brightly coloured of all marsupials. Unlike the terrestrial kangaroos, their limbs are more or less equal in proportions. They have rather large feet, and on their soles there are pads which undoubtedly help when climbing. Although the thickly furred tail is not prehensile it aids balance when climbing. Tree Kangaroos are very agile, they can make leaps of up to 9 m from tree to tree and jump to the ground from heights of at least 18 m without hurting themselves. They feed mostly on fruit and leaves. After a gestation of about 32 days a single young is born. They are rather slow growing, first emerging from the pouch at about 10 months, but continuing to suckle until nearly 14 months old. Matchei's Tree Kangaroo has lived up to 14 years in captivity. The rarest species are the Unicoloured Tree Kangaroo *D. dorianus*, which is now being bred in a few zoos, and Goodfellow's Tree Kangaroo which is bred in some numbers. Both are from New Guinea.

Goodfellow's Tree Kangaroo

WOMBAT *Vombatus ursinus*

The Wombat was once found over most of coastal regions of Australia from south-east Queensland to south-east Australia and Tasmania, including islands in the Bass Strait. Wombats look like small bears, growing to 1.2 m long and a weight of up to 35 kg. They occur mainly in forests in rocky habitats where they dig a complicated network of burrows, up to 30 m long, including a nesting chamber. Because of

Common Wombat

their burrowing activities – which can cause cattle and sheep to injure themselves – and because rabbits often share their burrows, Wombats have been exterminated over much of their range. They are nocturnal (though they occasionally sunbathe), and feed on grasses, roots, fungi and other vegetable matter. The single young (occasionally twins) is born into the mother's pouch and first ventures from the pouch after about 10 weeks, leaving the pouch complete 2½ weeks later, and is independent at about 10 months old. Because of persecution by man, Wombats are now extinct over much of their former range, including all the Bass Strait islands, except for Flinders' Island, but on Tasmania they are still reasonably abundant, particularly in the mountain forests. A Wombat has lived for over 26 years in captivity.

The Hairy-nosed Wombat *Lasiorhinus latifrons* is closely related to the Wombat but, as its name suggests, has a hairy nose, as well as larger, more pointed ears. They are generally similar in habits. However, the decline of the Hairy-nosed Wombats has been much more marked than that of the Wombat and it is now extinct in several areas. Both species are comparatively rare in captivity.

The Koala Bear *Phascalarctos cinereus* is a comparative rarity in zoos, only occasionally seen outside Australia. It was once on the verge of extinction due to hunting for its fur – over 2 million skins were being exported in one year alone. Fortunately protection from 1920 onwards has enabled them to recover.

LONG-NOSED POTOROO   *Potorous tridactylus*

The Potoroos are rat-like marsupials, with rather short hind feet, which gives them more of a galloping, running gait with kangaroo-like hops, but they can make leaps of 1.5 m high and 2.5 m long. The Long-nosed Potoroo is about 38 cm long, plus a tail of over 20 cm, and weighs around 1.5 kg. Potoroos are found in dense grassland or other comparatively damp forest areas, making nests under leaves and other forest litter in eastern and south-eastern Australia and Tasmania. They are mostly nocturnal, feeding principally on fungi, but also grass, roots and tubers and other vegetable matter, and in summer they also eat large numbers of insects. The females have two litters a year, giving birth to a single young after a gestation of 38 days. The young remains attached to the nipple inside the mother's pouch for 55 days, and leaves the pouch 75 days later. In the wild Long-nosed Potoroos are known to have lived over 7 years, and in captivity they have lived over 9 years.

A closely related species, the Broad-faced Potoroo *P. platyops* which was once found in south-western Australia became extinct around 1875, and a subspecies of the Long-nosed Potoroo *P. tridactylus gilberti* has not been seen since the beginning of the century; it formerly occurred in south-western Australia.

ANTEATERS

Giant Anteater

The Giant Anteater *Myrmecophaga tridactyla* was once found in open forest and savanna in South America from northern Argentina to Guatemala and Belize. Due to human disturbance and hunting it is now rare or even extinct over much of its former range. It grows up to about 1.2 m, plus a tail of 90 cm and weighs up to 39 kg. It feeds on termites and ants, ripping open the mounds with powerful claws and gathering ants, larvae and eggs with a long sticky tongue, eating up to 30,000 in one day; Anteaters also eat other insects occasionally. The remarkable tongue can be extended over 60 cm, but it is only 10–

15 mm across at its widest part. A single young is born after a gestation of about 190 days and is carried on the mother's back. A Giant Anteater has lived over 25 years in captivity.

There are two species of Tamanduas or Lesser Anteaters: *Tamandua tetradactyla*, which is found in South America east of the Andes from Venezuela to Uruguay, and *T. mexicana*, found from southern Mexico to Peru and Venezuela. They grow to a maximum of 77 cm plus a tail of up to 67 cm and weigh up to 7 kg. Tamanduas live in more forested areas than the Giant Anteater, and spend much of their life in trees where they are excellent climbers using their prehensile tails. They feed on ants and termites. Although popular zoo exhibits, Tamanduas are rarely bred in captivity. The Silky or Dwarf Anteater *Cylopes didactylus* is a rarity in zoos. It is found in forests from Mexico to Bolivia and Brazil, rarely, if ever descending to the ground.

Tamandua *Tamandua tetradactyla*

SLOTHS

Two-toed Sloth *C. hoffmanni*

Three-toed Sloth *B. tridactylus*

There are about 5 species of sloth (depending on their classification), all confined to Central and South America. They are exclusively tree dwelling and find it very difficult to walk on the ground. However, several extinct species of ground sloths are known, some of which may still have been in existence when the first Europeans visited the New World. The largest of the ground sloths were as big as elephants. The surviving sloths are all adapted to living upside down in trees, and their camouflage is enhanced by growths of algae on their fur.

There are 2 closely-related species of Two-toed Sloth: *Choloepus hoffmanni* found from Nicaragua, south to Ecuador, and *C. didactylus* found east of the Andes to the Amazon basin. They grow to a maximum of 74 cm, lack a tail, and weigh up to 8.5 kg. A particular peculiarity of the Two-toed Sloth, is that whereas most mammals consistently have 7 neck vertebrae, Two-toed Sloths have 6, 7 or 8. A single young is born after a gestation of up to $11\frac{1}{2}$ months (or much shorter). They breed freely in captivity and have lived over 31 years in zoos.

The 3 species of Three-toed Sloths have similar habits to the Two-toed: the Pale-throated Sloth *Bradypus tridactylus* is found in southern Venezuela, the Guiana and northern Brazil; the Brown-throated Sloth *B. variegatus* from Honduras to northern Argentina and the Maned Sloth *B. torquatus*, probably the rarest species, is found in the rapidly disappearing coastal forests of south-eastern Brazil, although the habitat of all is threatened.

ARMADILLOS

Nine-banded Armadillo

There are about 20 species of armadillo known, all found in the Americas. Most species are found in fairly open country, but the largest, the Giant Armadillo *Priodontes maximus* (up to 60 kg) is mainly forest dwelling. The smallest is the Fairy Armadillo *Chlamyphorus truncatus* and the most widespread the Nine-banded Armadillo *Dasypus novemcintus*, found from Uruguay northwards throughout Central America, into the USA. Since the beginning of this century the Nine-banded Armadillo has considerably expanded its range in the USA, partly as a result of deliberate introductions, and it continues to spread. It grows to about 70 cm and weighs up to 6.3 kg, but more normally 4 kg. The litter nearly always contains 4 young, born after a gestation of 4 months. A peculiar feature of their reproduction is that all the young in any particular litter come from a single fertilized egg, and are consequently all identical quads of the same sex. The life spans of armadillos are poorly known, but in the wild Nine-Banded Armadillos are believed to live up to 7 years.

The Three-banded Armadillo *Tolypeutes matacus*, is found in Bolivia, Brazil, Paraguay and Argentina, in open areas. Like the previous species it feeds largely on insects such as ants and termites. It normally gives birth to only a single young after a gestation of 120 days. The newborn young are miniatures of the adults, although the eyes and ears are not open, they are able to walk and roll up into a ball. Although armadillos are exhibited in many zoos and have been bred in laboratories, they are only rarely bred in zoos.

Armadillos are preyed on by many carnivores, but among their most important predators are cars, which cause considerable mortality. Their skins have also been used extensively in the curio trade for manufacture of folk 'guitars' and other souvenirs and their meat has also been important.

Three-banded Armadillo defensive posture

TENRECS

There are about 30 different tenrecs, all of which are confined to Madagascar. Tenrecs are small insect-ivores which have filled most of the ecological niches occupied by shrews, hedgehogs, moles and other small insectivores found in other parts of the world. There are aquatic species such as the rare Web-footed Tenrec *Limnogale mergulus*, and burrowing, mole-like species such as the Rice Tenrec *Oryzorictes talpoides*. The rarest is the forest-dwelling *Dasogale fontoynonti* which is only known from a single specimen. One of the commonest species is the rabbit-sized Tail-less Tenrec *Tenrec ecaudatus* which grows to about 35 cm and a weight of 3 kg. It is very prolific and litters of 12 are common, and up to 21 have been recorded. Like all tenrecs, it feeds on insects and other invertebrates and any small mammals it encounters. The Greater Hedgehog-tenrec *Setifer setosus* is only about one-third the size of a European Hedgehog, but is equally spiny and rolls into a ball when in danger. It is occasionally exhibited in zoos. The Lesser Hedgehog or Pygmy Tenrec *Echinops telfairi* is also sometimes seen.

Rural peoples sometimes hunted tenrecs for food

HEDGEHOGS

The Northern Hedgehog *Erinaceus europaeus* grows to about 25 cm long (its tail is small and concealed) and weighs around 800 g, increasing to 1400 g before hibernating. It is widespread and often common over most of north-western Europe, and in New Zealand, where it has been deliberately introduced. Two other similar species also occur in parts of Europe: the Algerian or Vagrant Hedgehog *E. algirus*, which is found in south-west Europe and North Africa, and the Eastern Hedgehog *E. concolor* of eastern Europe. Hedgehogs are mainly nocturnal and are found in a wide variety of habitats; and the European Hedgehog has adapted to many man-made ones. They feed on a

European Hedgehog

wide variety of invertebrates and other small animals, birds' eggs and reptiles (including poisonous snakes). The Northern Hedgehog has 2–9 young in a litter, born almost naked and with soft spines, after a gestation of 30–48 days. A second litter is occasionally produced, but the young from this are less likely to survive the winter hibernation. Hedgehogs are often kept in zoos but only comparatively rarely bred, and it is doubtful that there are any self-supporting captive populations. They have lived for 6 years or more in captivity, but are much shorter lived in the wild.

Several other species of hedgehog are sometimes exhibited in zoos, including the Long-eared Hedgehog *Hemiechinus auritus* which is found from eastern North Africa through Arabia to India and Mongolia.

The Moonrats of south-east Asia are related to hedgehogs but, although similar in many ways, lack the hard spines of true hedgehogs. Moonrats are rarely seen in captivity. The largest known insectivore is the Moonrat *Echinosorex gymnurus*.

Long-eared Hedgehog

COMMON TREE SHREW *Tupaia glis*

Tree shrews are among the largest of the insectivores and are of considerable interest to zoologists as they are often considered to be closely related to the ancestors of monkeys, apes and man, which probably looked similar to tree shrews. Although they are also related to shrews, in some ways they behave more like squirrels and their scientific name comes from the Malay *tupai*, which is used for any squirrel-like animal. All 16 of the tree shrews are found in India and south-east Asia. The Common Tree Shrew is the most widespread species, found from the Himalayas eastwards to southern China and south to the Malay Peninsula, Sumatra, Borneo and Java. It grows to 20 cm, plus a bushy tail of 19 cm, and weighs up to 185 g. Common Tree Shrews are mostly diurnal and live mainly in thick undergrowth and low bushes, where they are agile climbers. They are omnivorous, feeding not only on insects, including ants and termites, but on a variety of fruits and other plant matter which they hold in their front paws; their thumbs and first toes are opposable, enabling them to grip. They are also fond of water, drinking and bathing in the pools found in tree hollows. They defend territories against intruders of their own kind, often noisily. They build nests in tree holes or under logs and breed at all times of the year, with 1–3 young born after a gestation of up to 56 days; the young leave the nest when just over 1 month old. In some areas Common Tree Shrews are abundant and have adapted to man-made environments, even entering houses. They are the only kind of tree shrew normally seen in zoos but, although they are often exhibited, only a few zoos are breeding them successfully. Like many insectivores, tree shrews are comparatively short-lived in the wild, although they can live for 2 or more years in captivity.

FRUIT BATS

Relatively few bats are exhibited in zoos, mainly because they are mostly difficult to keep in captivity and are also rather difficult to present to the public. However, a few zoos, particularly those with nocturnal exhibits, now display them. Altogether there are over 950 known species of bats in the world, and probably many more await discovery in the tropical forests. The majority are rather small and most feed on insects. However, a few grow to a large size and feed mainly on fruit. There are about 170 fruit bats or flying foxes, the largest of which may weigh 1.2 kg

Egyptian Fruit Bat

and have a wing span of 1.7 m. Several species of fruit bat are occasionally seen in zoos, the most frequent being the Egyptian Fruit Bat *Rousettus aegyptiacus* and the Indian Flying Fox (p. 54). The Egyptian Fruit Bat is one of the smaller fruit bats, with a head and body length of about 12 cm, and weighs up to 170 g. It is widespread in many parts of Africa, through the Middle East (including Turkey and Cyprus) to Pakistan. Other closely related species are found in Africa, southern Asia and the western Pacific. Unlike most other fruit bats, *Rousettus* bats navigate by echolocation as well as by sight. They often roost in large colonies, with both sexes mixed together; up to 9000 have been found in a single roost. A single young (occasionally twins) is born after a gestation of about 4 months. When newly born they are carried clinging to the mother, until they become too heavy, when they are left hanging up in the roost. They are weaned at about 5–6 months old, when they start to fly. Egyptian Fruit Bats are often bred in captivity and some zoos have bred them for several generations.

Other species of fruit bat exhibited in zoos include the Straw-coloured Fruit Bat *Eidolon helvum* from Africa, Madagascar and Arabia which has been recorded in colonies of about 1 million individuals. Other than fruit bats, relatively few species of bat are exhibited in zoos. Occasionally vampire bats *Desmodus rotundus* are exhibited and have even been bred in captivity. They feed on the blood of mammals and birds.

INDIAN FLYING FOX *Pteropus giganteus*

Flying foxes are the largest of the bats and are mostly fruit eaters, less adapted to nocturnal life than most other bats. One of the largest species is the Indian Flying Fox or Greater Indian Fruit Bat, which has a wingspan of over 120 cm, although its head and body is only about 23 cm long and it weighs no more than 600 g. It is found from India eastwards to western China and south to Sri Lanka and the Maldive Islands. Indian Flying Foxes spend the day in noisy roosts in the tops of trees, and may even roost in the centre of large towns such as Delhi. At dusk they leave the roost in search of fruit, which they chew to extract juice and then spit out the pulp. They fly with characteristic slow wing-beats and may travel considerable distances to feed. They are regarded as a pest in some fruit-growing areas. A single young is born in early spring after a gestation of up to 150 days and clings to the mother until it is too big to carry. Although the Indian Flying Fox is not endangered, most of its close relatives have very restricted ranges and several are endangered; some may already be extinct. Those particularly threatened occur mostly on islands in the Indian and Pacific Oceans. Indian Flying Foxes are frequently exhibited in zoos; they adapt well to captivity and will often breed. Several other species are occasionally seen, and there is now a thriving colony of Rodrigues Flying Foxes *P. rodricensis*, an endangered species, in Jersey Zoo.

LEMURS (1)

Ring-tailed Lemur

Black Lemur

male

female

The Lemurs are confined to Madagascar. There are 4 families. Of the 7 species of mouse lemur, Cheirogalidae, only one is at all common in captivity, the Lesser Mouse Lemur *Microcebus murinus*. The leaping lemurs or indris and sifakas, Indriidae, are very rarely seen in captivity. The only member of the Daubentonidae, the Aye-aye *Daubentonia madagascariensis*, is a curious long-fingered nocturnal lemur which is on the brink of extinction. The remaining 16 lemurs belong to the family Lemuridae, and are the species most commonly exhibited in zoos. The Ring-tailed Lemur *Lemur catta* occurs in forested areas of southern Madagascar, it grows to a length of up to 45 cm plus a tail of 55 cm. It is less arboreal than most other species and consequently has a smaller first toe, since it is not used for gripping, and the soles of its feet are leathery. When walking on all 4 feet it holds its tail erect. Ring-tailed Lemurs live in groups of up to 24. A single young, (occasionally twins) is born after a gestation of about $4\frac{1}{2}$ months; the baby clinging to the underside of the mother until about a week old, when it climbs on to her back; females are mature at about 20 months, males 30 months. They have lived in captivity for at least 18 years, breed in large numbers each year and have been self-sustaining for many years. The Black Lemur *L. macaco* is found in north-western Madagascar, and as in several Lemurs, the sexes have different colouring. In general biology it is similar to the Ring-tailed Lemur. Several subspecies are exhibited in zoos, where they are often bred.

male Ruffed Lemur

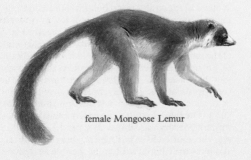

female Mongoose Lemur

The Ruffed Lemur *Varecia variegata* is the largest living true lemur, growing to a length of about 60 cm, plus a tail of about the same length, and weighs about 3 kg. Its extremely variable coat pattern may not even be symmetrical, and in colour ranges from jet black to bright rufous, with varying amounts of white. Ruffed Lemurs are arboreal, and leap from tree to tree, feeding mostly on fruit. They live in small groups, usually containing a pair of adults and their young. Twins, triplets or single young are born after a gestation of up to 102 days. When newborn the female may leave them in a tree while she feeds. They are climbing well by 5 weeks, are weaned at about 4½ months and females are mature at 20 months. Ruffed Lemurs are declining from loss of habitat in their native forests of eastern Madagascar. They are regularly bred in captivity and have lived for up to 19 years.

The Mongoose Lemur *Lemur mongoz* is found in north-western Madagascar and the Comoro Islands (where they were probably introduced long ago), and like most other lemurs is threatened by the destruction of its forest habitat. In some parts of their range Mongoose Lemurs are apparently nocturnal, but in others active by day. They live in small family groups, and are very noisy when they meet another group. Single young (occasionally twins) are born after a gestation of 128 days, and for the first week or so, the young clings to its mother's underside, and then is carried on her back. Mongoose Lemurs are seen in many larger zoos where they breed regularly.

LORISES

The Slow Loris *Nycticebus coucang* grows to about 30 cm and weighs up to 900 g; the tail is vestigal. It is found from the eastern Himalayas southwards through Assam and Burma to the Malay Peninsula, Sumatra, Java and Borneo. A closely related species, *N. pygmaeus*, occurs in Indochina. The Slow Loris is widespread and is often found in agricultural areas and even suburban gardens, though because of its nocturnal and arboreal habits it is rarely seen; during the day it sleeps in the fork of a branch. Its

Slow Loris

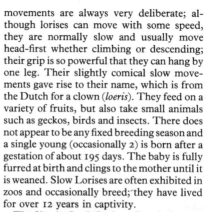

movements are always very deliberate; although lorises can move with some speed, they are normally slow and usually move head-first whether climbing or descending; their grip is so powerful that they can hang by one leg. Their slightly comical slow movements gave rise to their name, which is from the Dutch for a clown (*loeris*). They feed on a variety of fruits, but also take small animals such as geckos, birds and insects. There does not appear to be any fixed breeding season and a single young (occasionally 2) is born after a gestation of about 195 days. The baby is fully furred at birth and clings to the mother until it is weaned. Slow Lorises are often exhibited in zoos and occasionally breed; they have lived for over 12 years in captivity.

The Slender Loris *Loris tardigradus* is more rarely seen in zoos. Confined to the Indian subcontinent and Sri Lanka, it is smaller than the Slow Loris but similar in behaviour. It feeds mainly on small animals.

The 3 species of tarsiers, distant relatives of the lorises from south-east Asia, have even more spectacular eyes but are rarely exhibited in zoos.

Slender Loris

POTTO *Perodicticus potto*

The Potto grows to a length of 40 cm, with a tail of less than 10 cm; it weighs up to 1.5 kg. It is found in western and central Africa, south of the Sahara, and is almost exclusively arboreal and nocturnal. A most curious feature of the Potto are 4 sharp projections on the back of the neck. These are processes of the last 2 neck and first 2 chest vertebrae, which project as spines. The Potto is believed to use them as a defence, bending its head between its forelegs when attacked. Its thumbs and big toes are set at 180° to the rest of its

fingers and toes, giving a very powerful grip. It moves slowly and deliberately, walking on all fours, and occasionally hangs by its hind feet to reach food, which consists of fruit and other vegetable matter, including fungi and leaves, and also birds' eggs, molluscs, lizards, insects and any other small animals it can catch. Pottos are preyed on by a wide variety of nocturnal carnivores including Genets, Palm Civets, large snakes and Eagle Owls. They are normally solitary, except when breeding; and within its own territory each animal has favourite eating and sleeping places. A single young (occasionally twins) is born after a gestation of about 170 days. The baby is left clinging to dense foliage while its mother feeds until it is about 1 month old, when she carries it on her back; at about 3–4 months it begins to follow her. Males are independent at 6 months, females at 8 months. Pottos are fairly adaptable, and often live around human habitation and in forest edge habitats and secondary forest. They are frequently kept in zoos, particularly those with facilities for displaying nocturnal animals, and have lived for up to 11 years in captivity.

The Angwantibo or Golden Potto *Arctocebus calabarensis* is a close relative of the Potto, rather similar in general appearance, but smaller and lacking any tail. It is found in a small area north of the lower Zaire River, to south-eastern Nigeria.

GALAGOS

Greater Galago

There are 7 species of bushbaby or galago, all African, but only 2 are common in zoos: the Greater or Thick-tailed Galago, *Otolemur crassicaudatus* and the Senegal Bushbaby or Lesser Galago *Galago senegalensis*. The Greater Galago grows to about 45 cm, plus a tail of 50 cm, and weighs up to 1.8 kg. It is found south of the equator to the Tropic of Capricorn. The Senegal

Bushbaby is under half the size of the Greater Galago, growing to 20 cm plus a tail of 30 cm, and weighing 300 gm. It is widespread over much of Africa south of the Sahara, except for the extreme south and the Zaire River Basin. The smallest species, Demidoff's Galago *G. demidovi*, is even smaller, weighing about 100 gm, but is rarely seen in zoos. Three other species are also very occasionally seen – Allen's Galago *G. alleni*, the Western Needle-clawed Galago *Euoticus egantulus*, and *O. garnetti*, a close relative of the Greater Galago. Bushbabies are agile climbers and are often sociable; as their large eyes suggest, they are strictly nocturnal. They feed on a wide variety of plants and insects, and also on lizards, birds and other small animals. Up to 3 young are born after a gestation of nearly 150 days. Both the Greater Galago and the Senegal Bushbaby are frequently bred in zoos, where they have lived for up to 14 years.

Demidoff's Galago

DOUROUCOULI *Aotus trivirgatus*

The Douroucouli, Night Monkey or Owl Monkey
Aotus trivirgatus, is an almost entirely nocturnal
species found in Central and South America, from
Panama south to Paraguay. They live at altitudes of

up to 2100 m (6800 ft) and are found in a wide variety of forest habitats where they build daytime nests of twigs and leaves in hollows, clefts or among vines. Douroucoulis grow up to 37 cm long, plus a tail of up to 40 cm, and they weigh up to 1 kg. Their large owl-like eyes give them excellent nocturnal vision, and they are very agile leaping from branch to branch. Unlike many other South American monkeys, the Douroucouli's tail is not prehensile. They feed on fruit, nuts, berries, flowers, insects and other small animals. Douroucoulis live in small groups, usually consisting of a pair of adults and their young. They are very vocal – over 50 sounds are known, including a call lasting several seconds and resonated with a throat sac. A single young is born after a gestation of about 150 days, and is mature at about 2 years. Douroucoulis used to be popular as pets, and they are exhibited in many zoos, particularly those with a nocturnal house. They breed regularly, and have been bred through several generations; in captivity they have lived for over 13 years.

By contrast, three species of Titi monkeys *Callicebus* spp, which superficially resemble Douroucouli, although they are diurnal, are comparatively rare in zoos. The Masked Titi *C. personatus* is the rarest species in the wild, and none are known to be in zoos at the time of writing. The Dusky Titi *C. moloch* can be seen in a few zoos and is occasionally bred in captivity.

UAKARIS

The Red Uakari *Cacajao rubicundus* is found from the central Amazon region to Peru and Colombia, where it has a fairly restricted habitat, preferring mainly riverine forests where it lives in the tops of trees, rarely descending to ground level. It grows to a length of about 57 cm, plus a relatively short tail of about 15 cm. This short tail is related to the fact that although Red Uakaris are agile climbers they do not leap, they are the only species of monkey in South America to have only a short tail. Their ears are rather human-

Red Uakari

like in appearance. They live in colonies which may range from 10 to 100 or more monkeys, but more usually of 30–50. Although they are primarily fruit eaters they will also eat leaves, insects and other small animals. The females give birth to a single young every other year, which becomes mature when about 3 years old. Small numbers of Red Uakari are in zoos, where some are being bred, particularly in the USA. Uakari have lived for over 20 years in captivity.

The White or Bald Uakari *Cacajao calvus* is very closely related to the Red Uakari, the most obvious difference being that its fur is a whitish instead of the reddish-chestnut of the Red Uakari, but it still has a scarlet face, and many people consider this to be merely a subspecies. It is found in the Upper Brazilian Amazon. Both the Red and the White Uakari have become rare because of habitat destruction, and they have also been collected for the pet trade.

A third species, the Black-headed Uakari *C. melanocephalus* is found in the Amazonian forests of Brazil, Colombia and Venezuela. Although it is not quite as rare as the other species, it is likely to become endangered as its habitat comes under pressure. Only the occasional White and Black-headed Uakaris are likely to be seen in zoos.

The Uakaris are generally quieter than other monkeys: the noisiest of the South American primates are the Howler Monkeys, which are comparatively rare in zoos. Their name derives from their exceptional voice, particularly the male's, which can be heard by humans from up to 5 km away.

WHITE-FACED SAKI
Pithecia pithecia

The White-faced Saki is found in the Amazon basin in southern Venezuela, the Guianas and north-eastern Brazil. The White-faced Saki grows to a length of about 70 cm, plus a tail of 25 cm, and weighs up to 1.7 kg. They live in forests and rarely descend to the ground, but do occasionally feed among the lower branches of the forest. They feed on fruit and berries and other plant matter, and also small animals such as bats, and birds which they tear up and pull the skin off. They live singly, or in small family groups of up to 5, and have a very loud call. A single young is born after a gestation of about 163 days, and it reaches maturity at about 4 years. Sakis are said to become very tame and gentle in captivity and in zoos they have been known to live for nearly 14 years.

There are 3 other closely related species: *Pithecia albicans* from central Amazonia, *P. hirsuta* and the Hairy Monk Saki *P. monachus* from the Amazon Basin in Colombia, Ecuador, Peru and Brazil. None of these appears to be immediately threatened.

In addition to the 4 *Pithecia* Sakis there are 2 species of closely related *Chiroptes* Sakis. These have rather human looking faces. The White-nosed Saki *Chiroptes albinasus* is found from the Amazon River to the Mato Grosso and the Black-bearded Saki *C. satanus* from Venezuela to Brazil. They have well developed ruff-like beards, and rather thick brush-like tails. The White-nosed Saki is threatened by the destruction of its forest habitat.

BLACK-CAPPED OR BROWN CAPUCHIN
Cebus apella

The Black-capped Capuchin (and its close relatives) are intelligent and active, and used to be popular with travelling organ grinders. The males have beards, and this, together with their black-capped appearance led to them being likened to Capuchin monks – who also wore beards. The Black-capped Capuchin occurs in eastern Colombia and Peru, to Bolivia and Venezuela and the Guianas, and over most of Brazil to Paraguay. It is found in a wider range of habitats than any other New World monkeys, including almost all types of forest, up to an altitude of 2700 m (8775 ft). Capuchins are extremely agile climbers, and their prehensile tail is often carried curled under when they are climbing. They live in troops of up to 20 animals feeding largely on fruits, nuts and berries but also on bark, shoots, insects and other small animals and birds' eggs. A single young is born after a gestation of 180 days, and is carried by the mother, clinging to her fur. Females reach maturity at 4 years, males at 8 years. When properly cared for, Black-capped Capuchins thrive in captivity and they are bred regularly in most of the leading zoos, and have been bred through several generations. They can live for a considerable time in captivity – over 44 years is the record so far.

There are 3 other species of capuchin, all from South America: the Brown Pale-fronted Capuchin *Cebus albifrons*, the White-throated Capuchin *C. capucinus* and the Weeper Capuchin *C. nigrivittatus*. They are all exhibited in zoos, though not as frequently as the Black-capped Capuchin.

SQUIRREL MONKEYS

There are 2 very closely related species of Squirrel Monkeys: the Common Squirrel Monkey *Saimiri sciureus*, which is widespread in South America from Colombia to Paraguay, and the Red-backed Squirrel Monkey *S. oerstedi*, which is confined to Costa Rica and Panama. The Common Squirrel Monkey

Common
Squirrel
Monkeys

grows to a length of 36 cm plus a tail of 42 cm, and weighs about 1 kg; apart from the marmosets and tamarins, they are the smallest primates in South America. Squirrel Monkeys live in troops of up to 300 or more, in a wide variety of mainly forested habitats, where they feed on fruit, seeds and other plant matter, as well as insects and other small animals such as frogs and snails. They are the most gregarious of all South American primates and within the troops they divide into subgroups, and an extremely large number of sounds are made as they encounter one another. After a gestation of 152–172 days a single young is born, which is carried about clinging to the mother. They become independent at 1 year; females mature at 3 years, males at 5, and in captivity they have lived for over 12 years. Squirrel Monkeys have long been popular, not only in zoos but also as household pets and dressed in dolls clothes as street photographers' accessories – they were one of the favourite animals with organ grinders. During the 1960s and 1970s tens of thousands were involved in trade and large numbers were also used in biomedical experiments. The Red-backed Squirrel Monkey is endangered by loss of habitat, and until recently was also being exploited for trade. Spraying against yellow fever and malaria may also have harmed Squirrel Monkeys and other wildlife. There are a few small colonies of Red-backed Squirrel Monkeys in captivity, and the Common Squirrel Monkey is one of the commonest primates in zoos.

BLACK-HANDED SPIDER MONKEY
Ateles geoffroyi

The Black-handed or Geoffroy's Spider Monkey is found from southern Mexico, south through Central America to north-western Colombia. They are long-limbed with a long prehensile tail, growing to a length of 43 cm, plus a tail of over 50 cm and weighing up to 5 kg. They are nearly as agile as the Gibbons of Asia, and can swing through the trees using their tail as an extra limb, but normally run along the top of branches with the tail arched over the back. They live in comparatively large troops in a wide variety of forest habitats, including mangroves, where they are largely opportunistic feeders, eating a wide range of fruits, nuts and other plant matter, and also eggs, insects and other small animals. In the wild they are known to attack intruders by breaking off branches, weighing up to 5 kg, and hurl them down at the intruders. The single young is born after a gestation of about 230 days, and females become sexually mature at 4 years, males at 5 years. In captivity one has lived for 33 years.

There are 3 other species of spider monkey: the Long-haired Spider Monkey *Ateles belzebuth*, the Brown-headed Spider Monkey *A. fusciceps* and the Black Spider Monkey *A. paniscus*, all from northern South America. All the spider monkeys are threatened, and several populations are extremely rare, or even extinct. In addition to forest destruction they are collected for trade and have also been extensively hunted as human food. The Black-headed Spider Monkey is commonly seen in zoos, the others more rarely.

COMMON WOOLLY MONKEY
Lagothrix lagothricha

The Common Woolly Monkey is found in scattered populations in the forests of north-western South America up to altitudes of 3000 m (9750 ft). Although once numerous and widespread it is no longer 'common'. It is one of the largest South American monkeys, growing to 68 cm, plus a tail of up to 72 cm, and weighing up to about 10 kg. Its fur is short and soft and the underside of the long prehensile tail is bare. Woolly Monkeys live in humid forests in troops of up to 50 individuals. Although mainly arboreal, unlike many other South American primates, they occasionally descend to the ground, and walk on their hind legs, holding their arms out to balance. They are primarily vegetarian, feeding mainly on fruits, but also eat other vegetable matter and insects. A single young is born after a gestation of 225 days; females are sexually mature at 4 years and males after 5 years. A Woolly Monkey has lived for over 25 years in captivity. Woolly Monkeys are rather gentle and fairly slow moving. They have long been popular zoo animals and are exhibited in most larger zoos, but are being bred in only a few zoos.

The closely related Yellow-tailed Woolly Monkey *Lagothrix flavicauda* was seen in 1925 in a small area of forest in Peru, and then not seen again by biologists until 1974. It differs from the Common Woolly Monkey in having a yellowish band on the underside of the tail, and a whitish patch on its muzzle. Both Woolly Monkeys are declining due to both habitat loss and intensive hunting for human food.

MARMOSETS (1)

There are about 17 species of Marmosets and Tamarins, all found in Central and South America, and mostly in the Amazon region. They are the smallest primates, and the smallest of all is the Pygmy Marmoset *Cebuella pygmaea*, which grows to a length of 15 cm, plus a tail of nearly 23 cm, and weighs under 140 gm. Twins are usual, born after a gestation of about 20 weeks, and they mature at about 1½–2 years. Unlike many other Marmosets, the Pygmy does not appear to be endangered as it is well able to adapt to man-made and disturbed habitats, after the forest has been cleared.

The Lion Tamarin *Leontopithecus rosalia* is one of the world's rarest animals, and all 3 subspecies, the Golden Lion Tamarin *L.*

Pygmy Marmoset

Golden Lion Tamarin

rosalia rosalia the Golden-headed Lion Tamarin *L.r. chrysomelas*, and the Golden-rumped Lion Tamarin *L.r. chrysopygus*, are endangered, with possibly less than 300 altogether in the wild. The Lion Tamarin grows to about 33 cm, plus a tail of up to 40 cm, and weighs up to about 700 gm. The long silky 'mane' gives it its name. They live in small family groups and 1–3 young (usually twins) are born after a gestation of up to 132 days.

The largest and most widespread of the Marmosets are the Long-tusked Marmosets or Tamarins *Saguinus* spp. There are about 11 species, one or more of which are found in most parts of Central and South America. The White-lipped Tamarin *S. labiatus* is found in central Amazonian Brazil and the Red-handed Tamarin *S. midas* in northern Brazil and the Guianas.

Red-handed Tamarin

White-lipped Tamarin

MARMOSETS(2)

The 3 species of Short-tusked Marmosets or Titis are distinguished from the Tamarins or Long-tusked Marmosets by their short canine teeth, which are hardly longer than their incisors. Like most other marmosets they show considerable variation within each species; the most widespread is the Silvery Titi *Callithrix argentata argentata* which is found in central Brazil and eastern Bolivia, south of the River Amazon; the Black-tailed Marmoset *C., argentata melanura* is the most widespread subspecies occurring in rather dry cool parts of central Brazil; the White Marmoset *C. argentata leucippe* is a rare subspecies found only in a small area of Brazil. The Common Marmoset *C. jacchus* is widespread in eastern Brazil, but some of its subspecies such as the Buffy Tufted-ear or White-eared Marmoset *C. jacchus aurita* are extremely rare; however the Black-eared

Black-tailed Marmoset   Common Marmoset

Marmoset *C. jacchus pencillata* is still widespread and fairly abundant. The third species, the Santarem Marmoset *C. humeralifer* from the Amazon basin, is also rather rare. The Short-tusked Marmosets are all under 30cm, with tails of less than 40cm, and weigh less than 450gm. They live in groups of up to about a dozen and are active by day, spending the night in tree holes and crevices. They feed on small animals such as insects, lizards and frogs, on birds' eggs and on fruit. They bite through tree bark to feed on the sap and gums that ooze. 1–4 young are born after a gestation of up to 148 days. They have lived up to 16 years in captivity and several colonies are now flourishing in zoos. All 3 Short-tusked Marmosets are closely related, some interbreed and many hybrids have been born in captivity; they may well be a single rather variable species.

Black-eared Marmoset

White-eared Marmoset

MARMOSETS (3)

The only species of Marmoset found in Central America is the Cotton-top Tamarin *Saguinus oedipus* which is found from south-eastern Costa Rica and Panama south to northwestern Columbia. There are 2 sub-species, Geoffroy's Tamarin *S. oedipus geoffroyi* which is found over most of the range and the Pinche or Cotton-top Tamarin *S. oedipus oedipus* which is confined to north-western Columbia. The latter is particularly rare, and until recently was being heavily traded, with thousands being caught each year.

The Bare-faced Tamarin *S. bicolor* is found in a relatively small area in the northern part of the Central Amazon Basin, and it is not known precisely how rare it is. However, unlike the Cotton-top, which is common in captivity with large numbers bred each year, there are,

Cotton-top Tamarin

Geoffroy's Tamarin

at the time of writing, only a handful of Barefaced Tamarins in captivity. The Emperor Tamarin *S. imperator*, is found in the western parts of Brazil, Eastern Peru and northern Bolivia. Tamarins are similar in size to other marmosets, and normally live in woodlands, forests and other thickly vegetated areas, where they are arboreal rarely descending to the ground. They feed on a wide range of small animals as well as fruits and other plant matter. They normally live in small family groups, but some species sometimes may join together into bands of 10–20. The young, usually twins, are born after a gestation of about 140 days, and reach maturity at 1½–2 years. Both parents look after the young, which are carried around on the parents back until they are nearly 2 months old.

Bare-faced
Tamarin

Emperor Tamarin

MACAQUES (1)

The macaques are among the hardiest and most widespread of all the monkeys. There are about 13 species found in North Africa (and Gibraltar), southern and eastern Asia north to Japan, and south to the islands of South-east Asia. Most macaques are gregarious, living in troops numbering half a dozen to 100 or more. The structure of the troop is very carefully established and nowadays, in the better zoos, macaques are usually kept in large enclosures in groups of sufficient size for the social organisation of the troop to be observed. In the wild most macaque troops are constantly on the move, though they may move within a fairly restricted area.

The Celebes Macaque or Black Ape *Macaca nigra* is the most distinctive of all the macaques, and is confined to the Celebes and neighbouring Butung in South-east Asia. Unlike most other monkeys it is often carnivo-

Black Ape

Toque Macaque

rous, hunting other animals such as birds, lizards, and rodents in addition to the macaque's more usual diet of berries, fruits and nuts.

The Toque Macaque *M. sinica* is another species confined to an island – Sri Lanka. It is closely related and similar in appearance to the Bonnet Macaque *M. radiata* of southern India. The Toque is the smallest macaque, with a total length of about 1 m, of which the tail is half.

The Japanese Macaque *M. fuscata* is the most northerly of monkeys. Some live high in the Japanese alps on a diet of seeds and bark in a habitat covered in snow for much of the year.

Japanese Macaque

MACAQUES (2)

The Rhesus Macaque *Macaca mulatta* is one of the best known of all primates and was used in hundreds of thousands for the preparation of polio vaccine, and for other medical and scientific experiments, including flights into space. It is found from eastern Afghanistan through northern and central India to Burma and south-eastern China. It lives in a wide variety of habitats, from sea level, up to 2500 m (8200 ft), and in many parts of its range it is abundant, living in large troops around villages and towns, and around temples where it often enjoys total protection from molestation.

The Barbary Ape *M. sylvanus* is now found only in a few isolated populations in the Atlas mountains of north Africa where it is restricted to oak and cedar forests in the Atlas and other mountains. In Gibraltar, on the tip of

Rhesus Macaque

Spain, a semi-wild population has been maintained by the British Garrison since at least 1704. The population is kept at about 30, by exporting small numbers. It is the only macaque which lacks a tail.

The Pig-tailed Macaque *M. nemestrina*, which has a relatively short tail, is widespread in south-east Asia from Assam and Burma south to the Celebes and Borneo. It is one of the species most commonly seen in zoos and has been domesticated and trained to gather coconuts. Other macaques likely to be seen include the Stump-tailed Macaque *M. arctoides,* the Crab-eating Macaque *M. fascicularis,* and the endangered Lion-tailed Macaque *M. silenus.* Several populations of various species of macaque have been introduced in the Caribbean, Mauritius, Florida, Brazil, China and elsewhere.

Barbary Ape

Pig-tailed Macaque

WHITE-COLLARED MANGABEY
Cercocebus torquatus

Three distinctive subspecies are recognized in this rather variable species: the Sooty Mangabey *C.t. atys*, the most common in zoos, which is found from southern China to the Ivory Coast, the typical

White-collared Mangabey *C.t. torquatus*, found from south-east Nigeria to the Zaire River, and the White-crowned Mangabey *C.t. lunulatus*, which occurs in eastern Ghana. The names indicate the main differences between them: varying amounts of white on the head and neck. They are found in a wide variety of habitats, including forest and cultivated lands near the forest edge. Males grow to a length of nearly 70 cm, plus a tail of 80 cm, and weigh up to 12.5 kg; females are slightly smaller. The tail is slightly prehensile – though it cannot be used to grasp – and when walking on the ground is held upright or carried forwards over the back. White-collared Mangabeys live in noisy troops of up to 20, usually permanently based around favourite feeding and sleeping areas. Mainly terrestrial, they also climb, and feed on nuts and fruit, including coconuts, also consuming a wide variety of other vegetable matter, and raid crops, particularly groundnuts. A single young is born after a gestation of about 210 days. Mangabeys have lived for 20 years in captivity.

Of the 3 other mangabey species the White-cheeked Mangabey *C. albigena* and the Black or Crested Mangabey *C. aterrimus* are occasionally seen in zoos, but rarely the Tana River Mangabey *C. galeritus*. Seriously endangered due to destruction of its forest habitat, it is protected in the Tana River Primate Reserve, in Kenya.

White-cheeked Mangabey showing facial display

BABOONS

The Olive or Anubis Baboon *Papio anubis* grows to about 100 cm, plus a tail of up to 70 cm, and weighs up to 30 kg; females are smaller than males. It is found in Africa from the River Niger eastwards to Kenya and is closely related to several other species.

The Guinea Baboon *P. papio* is found in eastern Senegambia north to Mali and Mauritania; the Yellow Baboon *P. cynocephalus* occurs from Somali to Mozambique and Angola; the Chacma Baboon *P. ursinus* in South Africa, as far north as Zambia, and the Hamadryas Baboon *P. hamadryas* in north-east Africa and south-west Arabia. All except the

Olive Baboons

Hamadryas are rather similar, but the Hamadryas male has a very well developed mane and whiskers. Baboons live in troops, led by a dominant male, which may number 100 or more. Usually a single young is born after a gestation of up to about 190 days; it is weaned at 8 months and sexually mature after 4 years. Baboons are omnivorous and mostly live in open country, often near rocky ravines, and wander extensively. Many populations have been exterminated, particularly in northern parts of Africa. The Olive and Hamadryas Baboons are most commonly seen in zoos, where they often live for 30 or more years.

MANDRILL   *Mandrillus sphinx*

The Mandrill grows to about 95 cm, plus a tiny tail of less than 10 cm, and weighs up to 30 kg. It is found in West Africa, north of the Zaire River. The Drill *M. leucophaeus* is closely related to the Mandrill and is also found in West Africa. Both species live in forests, including dense rainforest, and also on agricultural lands, normally sleeping in the tops of trees. They feed on small animals, including termites, molluscs and rodents, birds, and a wide variety of vegetable matter. The most spectacular feature of the Mandrill is the highly coloured muzzle of the male, together with its bright blue posterior and scrotum contrast-

Mandrill

ing with its red penis. Mandrills and Drills do not mix, but both live in troops of up to about 20, consisting of a dominant male together with females and young. Sometimes troops gather together, into groups of 200 or more. The single young may be born at any time of the year, after a gestation of about 230 days. Mandrills are seen in most larger zoos, where they frequently breed, and have lived up to 46 years in captivity. The Drill is much more rarely seen.

A related and spectacular species of baboon, the Gelada Baboon *Theropithecus gelada*, found only in ravines in Ethiopia, is also exhibited more rarely in zoos; the males have thickly furred manes and impressive whiskers.

male Drill

SAVANNAH MONKEY *Cercopithecus aethiops*

South African
Vervet *C. aethiops
pygerythrus*

Tantalus
Monkey
*C. aethiops
tantalus*

Green Monkey
*C. aethiops
sabaeus*

Grivet *C. aethiops aethiops*

The Savannah Monkey (also known as the Vervet, Grivet, Tantalus Monkey and Green Monkey, depending on the subspecies) grows to a maximum of just over 80 cm, plus a tail of 115 cm, and weighs up to 2.5 kg; females are smaller than males. Very variable in colour and pattern, some 21 subspecies have been described. Savannah Monkeys are often found close to human habitation in open country throughout most of Africa south of the Sahara up to altitudes of 4000 m. They may be abundant in agricultural lands, where they can be serious pests, but are absent from rainforest and drier habitats. They feed on a variety of plants and small animals, as well as cultivated crops, and are prey for the larger cats, eagles, pythons, crocodiles and even baboons. They may live in troops of 100 or more, but usually in smaller family parties led by an old male. Like several other guenons, the male has a spectacular threat display exposing his erect red penis and blue or white scrotum in front of his white belly fur. After a gestation period of up to 200 days a single young (occasionally twins) is born which is clasped to the mother until about 10 days old, when it is able to hang on by itself. The young start to explore at 3 weeks, are suckled for 6 months and mature at about 2½ years: they have lived for 24 years in captivity. Savannah Monkeys have been exploited for bio-medical research and for the pet and zoo trade. Large numbers were also once killed for their fur. They are exhibited in most large zoos and breed regularly.

DIANA MONKEY *Cercopithecus diana*

Diana Monkeys are found in West Africa from Sierra Leone to Ghana. They are among the most colourful of the guenons and occur in 2 subspecies, the typical Diana *Cercopithecus diana* which is found from Liberia eastwards to the Ivory coast, and the Roloway Monkey *C.d. roloway*, which has more yellowish-orange thighs and lacks eartufts, and is found in Ghana and the Ivory Coast. Both subspecies live in rainforest where they are almost entirely arboreal, keeping to the canopy and upper levels and rarely descending to the ground. They are medium-sized, long-tailed guenon monkeys, growing to just under 50 cm, plus a relatively long tail of 80 cm; the males weigh up to 7.5 kg, the females being much lighter. Diana Monkeys live in troops of up to 30 and like other guenons they are omnivorous and also raid crops. They are preyed on by Leopards, Pythons and larger birds of prey. The young are born after a gestation of about 7 months are are suckled for 6 months, maturing at 4–5 years. They have lived for up to 19 years in captivity. The Diana Monkey has been exploited by trade in the past, but is now mainly threatened by loss of its forest habitat, the few remnants of which are disappearing at an alarming rate in West Africa.

Several other similar species of guenon are sometimes seen in zoos, including L'Hoest's Monkey *C. lhoesti*, from Central Africa and the Mona Monkey *C. mona*, from West Africa. In Zaire there are some little known populations of guenons, some of which may be separate species. The striking colours and patterns of the guenons are thought to help species recognition in the gloom of the forest, where they see each other only in brief glimpses.

DE BRAZZA'S MONKEY
Cercophithecus neglectus

De Brazza's Monkey, or the Chestnut-browed Guenon, grows to 60 cm, plus 85 cm of tail, and weighs up to 8 kg. Females are much smaller than males. It is found from south-eastern Gabon, through the Zaire River basin to Uganda, Kenya and Sudan, usually near water and mainly in forests, including rainforest, where they are agile climbers, and in swamps. De Brazza's Monkeys usually live in groups, or occasionally in larger troops of up to 40 animals which contain several families. Active in the morning and afternoon, they often descend to the ground to feed on a wide variety of plant matter, including leaves, shoots and berries, as well as on insects and lizards. They often raid crops and frequently mix with Savannah Monkeys (p. 97) when feeding. They are preyed upon by leopards, eagles and pythons and are sometimes persecuted by man for raiding crops. A single young is born after a gestation of about 180 days; it can clamber around on its own when 3 weeks old. Like other guenons, De Brazza's has complex displays. The male's threat display is similar to that of vervet monkeys: it first consists of sitting with his legs splayed to expose red penis and blue scrotum, contrasting with his white thighs; when really excited he stands up and spreads his white beard, exposes all of his white underside, and bobs up and down. De Brazza's Monkey is exhibited in most larger zoos and breeds regularly in many American ones.

The Diademed Monkey *C. mitis*, also known as Sykes' Monkey, Blue Monkey or the White-throated Monkey depending on the subspecies, is similar in appearance to De Brazza's, but lacks white on the thigh and has more white on the side of the face, Various subspecies of this monkey are exhibited and occasionally bred in captivity.

PATAS MONKEY *Erythrocebus patas*

Male Patas Monkeys grow to about 75 cm, plus a tail of the same length, and weigh up to 13 kg; females are nearly half the size of males. They are very slender, long-limbed, long-tailed monkeys found in open country such as savannah and grassy plains, and occasionally also in forest areas and around human settlements and near rivers. They range across Africa south of the Sahara from Senegal to the Sudan, and south as far as Kenya. Patas Monkeys live in small

troops of up to 20, led by an old male, occasionally more, and wander extensively – a troop may travel 12 km in a day. They are almost entirely terrestrial and while the troop forages the old male usually stands sentinel – often on a termite mound. When alarmed a Patas Monkey can run in short bursts at speeds of up to 50 kph (30 mph); when running they hold the tail curved over the body. They feed on a wide variety of seeds, fruits, roots, insects, lizards and ground-nesting birds and their eggs. They are, in turn, preyed upon by hyenas, Leopards, eagles and formerly by Cheetahs and Hunting Dogs (both of which are now extinct over most of the Patas Monkey's range). A single young is born, usually between December and February, after a gestation of about 170 days. The young clings tightly to its mother at first, begins to explore on its own at about 2 weeks, but is carried until 3 months old; sexual maturity is reached at about 3½ years. Surplus males sometimes form separate troops or live singly. Patas Monkeys have been involved in trade extensively in the past, less so in recent years. Most of the trade is now for bio-medical research, but a substantial number were once captured for zoos and as pets. They are still frequently exhibited in zoos and regularly bred, occasionally through more than one generation, and have lived for up to 20 years in captivity.

COLOBUS

Black Colobus *C. satanus* Angolan Black-and-white Colobus

Gueraza

Olive Colobus *Procolobus verus*

Red Colobus *Colobus badius*

The male Black-and-white Colobus *Colobus polykomos* grows to just over 65 cm, plus a tail of up to 90 cm and a weight of 20 kg; females are slightly smaller. The proportions of black and white fur vary enormously over their range, which extends through the forests of West and Central Africa to Angola and Kenya. They are strictly arboreal, living and feeding mainly in the forest canopy. They make enormous leaps and to escape danger they plunge down to the lower levels of the forest using the springiness of the branches to catapult them to safety. They live in small family groups led by a male, feeding mainly on leaves, together with bark, seeds and insects. They breed all the year round and the single white young is born after a gestation of up to 178 days. The baby begins to explore and jump at 3 weeks but still returns to the mother when in danger until about 1 year, females are mature at 2 years, males at 4. They have lived up to 20 years in captivity, but relatively few zoos have been really successful in keeping colobus, and only a handful breed them.

The similar Gueraza *C. guereza* and Angolan Colobus *C. angolensis* are occasionally seen in zoos, but the various reddish brown species of Colobus *C. badius*, *C. kirki* and the Black Colobus *C. satanus* are rarely seen. Colobus fur has been (and still is) used for coats, trimmings and the regalia of African chiefs while loss of forest habitat threatens or endangers many populations.

LANGURS (1)

Common Langur

Dusky Langur

There are about 16 species of langur found in India and Sri Lanka, and south-east Asia south to Borneo, Java and Sumatra. One of the best known and most widespread is the Common Langur or Hanuman Monkey *Presbytis entellus*, which is found as far north as Tibet, Nepal and Kashmir and south in India, Bangladesh and Sri Lanka. It lives in a wide variety of habitats from sea level to over 4000 m (1300 ft). It grows to about 75 cm plus a tail of up to 100 cm, and may weigh up to 21 kg (in the Himalayas). Over much of its range it is venerated by Hindus and therefore seldom molested and lives close to human habitations and raids farms and gardens. Common Langurs normally live in troops of up to about 25, but occasionally 100 or more, led by a male. The females give birth to a single young (sometimes twins) every other year, after a gestation of up to 210 days. The young are weaned at 10–12 months and mature at 4 years (females) and 6–7 (males). In captivity a Common Langur has lived over 25 years.

The Dusky Langur also known as the Spectacled Leaf Monkey *P. obscura*, is also likely to be seen in zoos. It is found in the Malay Peninsula and some nearby islands. It grows to about 68 cm plus a tail of up to 80 cm and weighs up to nearly 7 kg. The newborn young are fully-furred but very different from the adults in coloration – they have pale orange fur and pink faces. Several langurs are seriously threatened, notably the Golden Langur *P. geei*, the Capped Langur *P. pileata*, the Nilgiri Langur, *P. johni* and François' Monkey *P. francoisi* and the Purple-faced Langur *P. vetulus*.

Douc Langur

Proboscis Monkey

The 2 species illustrated are not true langurs *Presbytis* spp (see p. 107), but close relatives: the Douc Langur *Pygathrix nemaeus* and the Proboscis Monkey *Nasalis larvatus*.

The Douc Langur is found in Indo-China and Hainan in tropical rainforest up to an altitude of 2000 m (6500 ft). It grows to a length of up to 76 cm, and has a tail up to 76 cm long. There is some variation in colour: the subspecies *P. nemaeus nemaeus* has a yellow face and white whiskers, while *P. nemaeus nigripes* has a black face. Because of the effects of the Vietnam War on its habitat and also because of extensive hunting for food the Douc Langur is now very rare.

The most noticeable feature of the Proboscis Monkey is its protruding nose, which in old males becomes very large. It is found on the island of Borneo, usually near water in lowland forests, including mangroves. It feeds almost exclusively on leaves together with some flowers and fruits. They are good swimmers and when disturbed they will plunge from a considerable height into water. The Proboscis Monkey grows to a length of up to 76 cm, plus a tail of 76 cm; males are larger than females and may weigh up to 22 kg – twice the weight of a female. They live in troops of up to about 30 animals. A single young is born after a gestation of about 166 days, and one has lived in captivity for over 13 years. Proboscis Monkeys were once considered very difficult to keep alive, but now thrive and have bred in several collections.

COMMON GIBBON *Hylobates lar*

The Common Gibbon (also known as the Lar, White-handed, Dark-handed, Silvery and Grey Gibbon, depending on the subspecies) once occurred throughout the forests of south-east Asia from Burma south through the Malay Peninsula to Sumatra, Java and Borneo. Now, with the disappearance of much of its forest habitat, its range is fragmented into isolated pockets with many of its populations extinct or rare. Common Gib-

bons have a head and body length of up to 50 cm (they lack a tail) and weigh about 4–5½ kg. A single young is born after a gestation of 7 months and carried by the mother until weaned at 4–7 months. They mature at 6–8 years and females bear young every 2–4 years; one has lived over 31 years in captivity. They live in small family groups proclaiming their presence at daybreak with a chorus of calls, even in zoos. Their normal method of locomotion is by 'brachiating' with their long arms. They can cover 3 m in a single swing, and leap over 9 m.

Other species to be seen in zoos include the Crested or Black Gibbon *H. concolor* and the Pileated Gibbon *H. pileatus*. All Gibbons are threatened, primarily by habitat loss but also by trade and hunting.

SIAMANG *Hylobates syndactylus*

The Siamang is the largest of all the gibbons with a head and body length of up to 90 cm and weighing up to 13 kg. Like all gibbons they are tailless. It is found in Malaya, in the forests of the hills of the centre of the peninsula, up to altitudes of 1800 m, and in the forests of Sumatra. An unusual anatomical feature is that the second and third toes are joined by a web of skin. They spend most of their day 25–30 m up in trees, feeding mainly on leaves and fruit, with small quantities of other plant matter and insects. They live in small family groups consisting of adults and their immature offspring. In common with other gibbons Siamangs are highly territorial and vocal, having territories which average just over 20 ha. The single young is born after a gestation of up to 235 days. At birth they are almost naked, but covered with fur a week later, and the mother carries her baby continuously for about 4 months. They do not mature until 8–9 years, and have been known to live 25 years in the wild. Like other gibbons, Siamangs have become very much rarer in the last few decades with the fragmentation and destruction of their forest habitats. By the year 2000 it is likely that they will only survive in a few National Parks and reserves, and in a few remaining forests inaccessible to commercial logging interests. Siamangs can be seen in many zoos. They are now being bred regularly and a few second generation young have been bred.

ORANG-UTAN *Pongo pygmaeus*

The Orang-utan is now confined to small areas of Sumatra and Borneo but until recently was much more widespread and during the Stone Age was found in south-east Asia from Peking to the Celebes. Remains at sites in Borneo suggest they have been kept as pets since prehistoric times. Orangs are

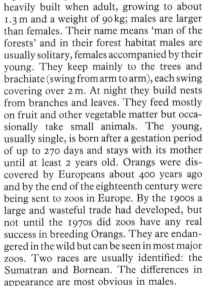

heavily built when adult, growing to about 1.3 m and a weight of about 90 kg; males are larger than females. Their name means 'man of the forests' and in their forest habitat males are usually solitary, females accompanied by their young. They keep mainly to the trees and brachiate (swing from arm to arm), each swing covering over 2 m. At night they build nests from branches and leaves. They feed mostly on fruit and other vegetable matter but occasionally take small animals. The young, usually single, is born after a gestation period of up to 270 days and stays with its mother until at least 2 years old. Orangs were discovered by Europeans about 400 years ago and by the end of the eighteenth century were being sent to zoos in Europe. By the 1900s a large and wasteful trade had developed, but not until the 1970s did zoos have any real success in breeding Orangs. They are endangered in the wild but can be seen in most major zoos. Two races are usually identified: the Sumatran and Bornean. The differences in appearance are most obvious in males.

male from Sumatra

male from Borneo

male with young

CHIMPANZEES

The Chimpanzee, *Pan troglodytes*, grows to a standing height of up to 170 cm and a weight in the wild of 55 kg (more in captivity); females are smaller than males. Formerly found in a wide variety of forest and more open habitats throughout West Africa south of the Sahara as far east as western Tanzania and south to the Zaire river, the Chimpanzee's range has become very much reduced and fragmented.

South of the Zaire River, the closely related Pygmy Chimpanzee or Bonobo, *P. paniscus*, is found.

Chimpanzees are social animals living in troops of up to 60 or more but usually in smaller family bands. They feed on a wide variety of plants and animal life, and have learned to use tools such as stones for breaking nuts, leaves for soaking up water and sticks

adult

adult

juvenile

for extracting termites from holes; this behaviour is not instinctive and has to be learnt from experienced animals. The young – usually 1 but twins are not uncommon – are born after a gestation of about 230 days. The baby first walks at about 6 months and separates from mother at about 4 years. In captivity Chimpanzees have lived up to 50 years. They are exhibited in most zoos and have been shown in circuses and other menageries and even kept as pets; when fully grown, however, they are often extremely aggressive and dangerous. They breed regularly in captivity, but relatively few zoos keep Chimpanzees in social groups as they occur in the wild, and only a few zoos have Pygmy Chimpanzees.

Chimpanzee

Pygmy Chimpanzee

GORILLA *Gorilla gorilla*

Lowland Gorilla female with young

The largest of the apes, male Gorillas grow to a height (when standing) of up to 180 cm, and a weight of 200 kg; females are usually much smaller. Gorillas are found in two separate areas: in West Africa, north of the Zaire River, and in eastern Zaire, Rwanda and Uganda (the Mountain Gorilla). They occur mainly in rainforest with dense undergrowth, and feed almost entirely on vegetable matter, particularly leaves and shoots, fruit and tubers. Gorillas live in troops led by a dominant male and containing up to 30 or more animals of a wide range of ages. A single young (exceptionally twins) is born after a gestation of about 257 days; it is weaned at about 1 year, but lives with its mother for about 3 years. Gorillas are declining throughout most of their range in the wild and the Mountain Gorilla is now reduced to a few hundred. They did not breed in captivity regularly until the 1960s and even now few zoos maintain natural groups. They have lived for up to 35 years in captivity.

Adult males

Mountain Gorilla

Lowland Gorilla

GOLDEN JACKAL   *Canis aureus*

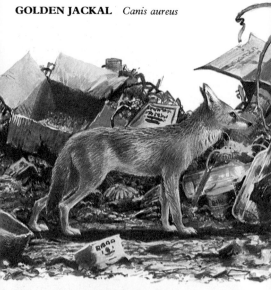

The Golden or Asiatic Jackal is rather like a small Alsatian (German Shepherd) Dog, growing to a height of about 40 cm and a length of up to 100 cm, plus a tail of about 25 cm, but there is considerable size variation. They can weigh up to 15 kg, but are usually lighter. Widespread in southern Asia from Asia Minor through the Middle East, throughout

India and eastwards to south-eastern Thailand and Burma, it also extends into south-eastern Europe and is widespread in northern Africa. It is found in a wide variety of habitats, being extremely adaptable, from tropical forest to dry plains and deserts and at altitudes of over 2000 m in the Himalayas. Golden Jackals are also often found associated with man, scavenging on refuse in and around villages and towns, hiding up by day in scrub and holes in the ground. They are usually nocturnal, hunting and scavenging alone, but sometimes banding together in packs. There are usually 3–8 cubs in a litter, born after a gestation of about 60 days; they suckle for 6 weeks and are sexually mature at about 10 months. Jackals can be extremely vocal and have a very wide variety of howls, barks, screams and whines, which are often made in chorus with other jackals. Golden Jackals are the species most commonly seen in zoos and are often bred in captivity.

In Africa, 3 other species of jackal also occur: the Side-striped Jackal *C. adustus*, the Black-backed Jackal *C. mesomelas* and the Simien Jackal *C. simensis*, a fox-coloured jackal, found only in a tiny area of Ethiopia, which is now endangered but not kept in any zoos.

The Dhole or Asian Wild Dog *Cuon alpinus* is another type of dog found in southern Asia. The disappearance of its forest habitat makes it increasingly scarce: it is only rarely seen in zoos.

WOLF *Canis lupus*

The Wolf is rather similar to jackals and German shepherd dogs, growing up to 160 cm, including tail of up to 45 cm, and weighing up to 72 kg (but usually less). It is very variable in appearance, ranging from heavily built, thickly furred animals in the north to rather small rangy animals in desert areas in the south. The Coyote *Canis latrans* of North and Central America is very similar in appearance but smaller, and the very rare Texan Red Wolf *C. rufus* is nearly extinct. The Wolf was once found in most habitats throughout the northern hemisphere, from Europe, including the British Isles, eastwards through Asia and India to Japan, and throughout North America as far south as Mexico. After centuries of persecution, however, it is now extinct or endangered over most of its range, and the few remaining populations are under pressure from fur trappers. The Wolf is the ancestor of the domestic dog, and in some areas the two still interbreed, giving very wolf-like breeds such as the Husky. Wolves hunt in small packs and feed on a wide variety of mainly mammal prey up to the size of deer and moose. They are frequently exhibited in zoos, but most are of unknown or mixed ancestry, as wolves have been regularly bred in captivity for over 100 years.

Wolf

Coyote

DINGO *Canis familiaris dingo*

The Dingo is a medium-sized, smooth-coated dog, usually sandy coloured, from Australia. It is not native to Australia, but was taken there by aboriginal colonists, probably before 15,000 BC. In many ways the Dingo, which is about 65 cm long and has a short tail, is similar to the Asiatic Wolf, which was undoubtedly its ancestor.

The New Guinea Singing Dog *C.f. hallstromi* is also closely related to the Dingo, and both are similar to the semi-wild Pariah dogs of India and southern Asia. Dingos and Pariah dogs frequently interbreed with domestic dogs and occasionally with wild

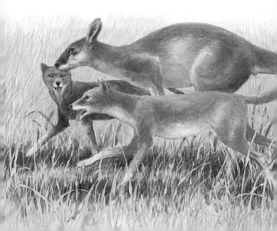

species such as wolves where they occur together, although the breeding biology of the Dingo and some other wild dogs differs from that of the domestic dog in that they only produce one litter a year of 4–8 pups, and they do not normally bark. When the European colonists arrived in Australia, Dingos were common, feeding mainly on marsupials such as kangaroos and wallabies, which they hunted in packs. The Australian aboriginals took young puppies from dens to rear as pets, but did not apparently breed them. After 2 centuries of persecution by sheep farmers, and constant interbreeding with domesticated breeds, the pure-bred Dingo is now becoming very rare. It is commonly kept and bred in many zoos, and occasionally kept as a pet.

Dingos hunting Red Kangaroo

ARCTIC FOX   *Alopex lagopus*

Arctic Foxes occur widely all around the polar regions in both the Old and New Worlds from Alaska to Siberia, as well as on most northern islands, including Greenland, Iceland and Spitsbergen, and the islands in the Bering Sea; in winter they may wander southwards, often covering long distances. They are fairly small, growing to a total length of about 90 cm, of which the tail is about one-third, standing about 30 cm at the shoulder and weighing up to 9 kg. There are 2 distinct colour phases, which may occur side by side, even in the wild. In one the summer coat is brownish and turns white in winter, while in the other phase it is brownish-grey in summer and smokey bluish-grey in winter. Since they live in the Arctic, Arctic Foxes are active by day or night, depending on the time of the year. They feed on a wide variety of animals including lemmings, voles, waterfowl and sea-birds, as well as scavenging the kills of other predators; they hide surplus food. Arctic Foxes are sociable, often living in large family groups, in extensive burrows which they excavate themselves or in natural rock crevices. They have 2 litters a year of up to 6 dark brown cubs, born after a gestation of 56 days. The litter size depends on the food supply. Arctic Foxes are exhibited in many zoos and occasionally bred. They have been ranched successfully on fur farms, and extensively traded. Despite the enormous numbers that are trapped for their fur, they are still widespread and abundant and do not appear to be endangered.

Adult, summer

Adult, winter

blue form

127

RED FOX *Vulpes vulpes*

The Red Fox is, throughout most of its range, one of the most abundant larger predators. It is widespread throughout the northern hemisphere as far south as the southern states of the USA, and in North Africa as far south as the Nile Valley; it has also been introduced into Australia. The North American Fox is sometimes regarded as a separate species, *Vulpes fulva*, and there are several other closely related species which are similar to the Red Fox. These include the Cape Fox *V. chama* from South Africa, the Pale Fox *V. pallida* and the Sand Fox *V. rueppelli*, both from around the Sahara; and the Bengal Fox *V. bengalensis* from India. The Red Fox grows to a total length of up to 120 cm, of which the tail is about one-third, and may weigh up to 10 kg. It normally breeds in underground earths and has 3–8 (max. 13) cubs after a gestation of up to 56 days. It is an opportunistic feeder, taking a wide variety of animals including mice, earthworms, ground-birds and frogs, but particularly voles; it also scavenges. Red Foxes have adapted to man-made environments and are often found in suburban and urban areas. They have been bred in captivity extensively, particularly in North America where a variety of colour variations such as silver fox and cross-fox have been especially bred for the fur industry. Surprisingly few Red Foxes are exhibited in zoos.

FENNEC FOX   *Vulpes zerda*

The Fennec Fox is a small, large-eared (up to 15 cm long) desert-living species, found in the Sahara and other arid areas of north Africa, and also in small areas of northern Arabia. It grows to a maximum of about 60 cm, of which the tail is about one-third, and weighs up to 1.5 kg. Its fur is very thick and soft and the soles of its feet are covered with hairs. The fur has occasionally been used in the fur industry, but not on a large scale. The Fennec Fox is nocturnal, hiding in a burrow during the day and emerging in the cool of evening and night to feed on lizards, insects and small mammals, as well as on birds' eggs, berries and other vegetable matter; like other foxes it hides surplus food. It is capable of surviving with little or no drinking water. Family groups live together and are very sociable. A single litter each year, of 1–5 young born after a gestation of about 50 days, reaches maturity at 6 months. They have lived for up to 11 years in captivity. Since their habitat is expanding numbers are probably increasing rather than declining. Fennec Foxes are popular exhibits in zoos which have facilities for showing nocturnal animals and breed fairly readily in captivity.

In Africa lives another desert-living species with even larger ears: the Bat-eared Fox *Otocyon megalotis*. In North America 2 small foxes occur in desert and open grassland habitats, the Kit Fox *V. macrotis* and the Swift Fox *V. velox*; only the Kit Fox has large ears.

RACCOON-DOG
Nyctereutes procyonoides

The Raccoon-dog was originally found only in the Far East, from Indo-China to Siberia and Japan, but as a result of deliberate introductions and escapes from fur farms it is now widespread over much of the USSR and eastern and central Europe, and its spread is still continuing. However, it has become rare in Japan and other eastern parts of its range. The Raccoon-dog is a true dog, but has a superifical resemblance to the Raccoon (p. 154) particularly in its facial markings. It originally occurred in mainly forested country, but it has adapted to a wide variety of other habitats and often occurs near water or close to man. Raccoon-dogs are omnivores, feeding on many different animals and plants, including insects, molluscs, crustaceans, reptiles, amphibians, small mammals, ground-nesting birds, fruit, berries, and carrion when available. They are mainly active in twilight or at night, and during daylight hours they hide away in a den which is usually in a rock cleft, burrow, hollow tree, or even in dense vegetation. The litter is born after a gestation of about 67 days and is large – sometimes up to 16 but more usually 6 or 7 cubs. The adults grow to about 80 cm, including a short bob-tail of about 15 cm, and a weight of up to 10 kg, more at the beginning of hibernation. During the winter months they may hibernate in the colder parts of the range, the cubs hibernating together with the adults. Raccoon-dogs are commonly seen in zoos and are frequently bred. They have been extensively bred on commercial fur farms and have lived for over 10 years in captivity.

MANED WOLF *Chrysocyon brachyurus*

The Maned Wolf is an impressive-looking species
with striking russet fur and exceptionally long legs;
with its white-tipped tail it looks rather like a long-
legged Red Fox. It grows to a length of 130 cm, plus a
tail of nearly 40 cm, and a weight of up to 23 kg. Its
name comes from the especially long hair on its neck
and back which can be made to stand on end. It is
found in open woodlands, grasslands and marshy
areas of South America, in southern Brazil and

Paraguay and northern Argentina. The Maned Wolf feeds on surprisingly small prey, including insects, snails, rodents, birds and amphibians, and also, more rarely, larger animals up to the size of sheep. It is very secretive, and nocturnal. Maned Wolves are very vocal, howling loudly and also barking; they snarl at each other rather like cats. Little is known of their breeding in the wild. The long legs are probably an adaptation for enabling Maned Wolves to see over tall grasses in open plains – similar to Cheetah and Serval Cats. In captivity, there are usually 1–5 cubs, born after a gestation of about 65 days. Maned Wolves are exhibited in many major zoos, and in recent years they have been bred fairly regularly; they have lived up to 13 years in captivity.

Several other dogs are also found in various parts of South America, including 7 species of Grey Foxes and Zorros *Dusicyon* spp. and the Bushdog *Speothos venaticus*.

AFRICAN HUNTING DOG   *Lycaon pictus*

The African Hunting Dog is a rather long-legged animal, growing to a length of up to 100 cm, plus a tail of up to 40 cm, and a weight of up to 36 kg, but often much less. Its colour and pattern are extremely variable, ranging from almost pure yellowish to entirely black, but the tip of the tail is always white; no two animals are exactly alike. It was once widespread over most of Africa including the Sahara and Egypt, but is now extinct over much of its former range, surviving only south of the Sahara, and even within this range its populations are increasingly fragmented and scattered. African Hunting Dogs are nomadic and travel in packs, usually of 4–6 but up to 100 have been recorded. They hunt a wide variety of

comparatively large game, including antelope and zebra foals, which they chase and eventually out-distance at speeds of up to 55 kph (35 mph). After a gestation of about 72 days, 2–16 cubs are born, usually in a burrow; there are normally twice as many males in a litter as females. Normally only the dominant female has cubs and if another gives birth the dominant one will often kill them. The cubs are suckled for up to 12 weeks and reach sexual maturity at 18 months; when the females become mature they usually leave the pack and join another. In the wild they live for 10–12 years. The African Hunting Dog has been persecuted by man and also appears to have been devasted by disease; it is probably one of the most critically threatened species of carnivores. Many zoos exhibit them and they are bred in small numbers in most years.

SPECTACLED BEAR *Tremarctos ornatus*

The Spectacled Bear is the only bear found in South America, where it once occurred in forest areas from Panama and Venezuela to Bolivia and Peru, and possibly in Argentina and Brazil. It grows up to 1.8 m long, plus a short tail of 7 cm, and has a shoulder height of up to 80 cm; it weighs up to 175 kg, but usually much less. Spectacled Bears live in a variety of mainly forest habitats at altitudes of up to 3100 m (11,800 ft), and are mainly nocturnal, hiding in hollow trees, among roots or in rocky clefts by day. They are mainly vegetarian, feeding on fruits and other vegetable matter, in particular bromeliads, and also insects, rodents and other animals. Other

favourite foods include palm hearts, and cacti fruit – they climb large cacti to reach them – and in some areas they have taken to raiding crops, particularly maize. A litter of 1–3 young is born after a gestation of 6.5–8.5 months. The young weigh only about 320 gm at birth and the mother remains with them in the den for several months. In captivity one has lived for over 36 years. However, in addition to forests they also occur in such diverse habitats as the treeless alpine zones of the Andes over 4000 m, and the coastal deserts with cacti. Although there are Spectacled Bears in many of the world's zoos, and they are now breeding regularly, at the time of writing none had bred them for more than one generation. In the wild, they are one of the world's rarest bears. Like most other species of bear they have been sought after as trophies by hunters, and in northern Peru (and possibly elsewhere) they have been hunted for their pelts and also for their fat and meat. They are also alleged killers of livestock – though this is unlikely. An increasing amount of their forest habitats are threatened, but with their adaptability and the inaccessibility of some of their habitats, and given some protection, particularly from hunting, there is no reason why they should not survive. However in many of these areas, which are rather barren, the bears need extremely large territories and in many formerly remote areas modern roads are being constructed which will give hunters access.

ASIATIC BLACK BEAR
Selenarctos thibetanus

The Asiatic Black Bear is found from Afghanistan eastwards through the Himalayas to China and Japan, and south to Burma. Its range overlaps with that of the Sloth Bear, and with the larger Brown Bear (p. 142) in the north and much smaller Sun Bear (p. 146) in the south-east. The Asiatic Black Bear is easily distinguished from the American Black Bear by a pale, whitish or yellowish V-shaped band across its chest. The American Black Bear *Ursus americanus* was formerly widespread throughout most of the wooded areas of North America, but although still locally abundant has a much reduced range. The Asiatic Black Bear, like most other bears is found mainly in montane woodlands and forests (up to 3600 m), but in some areas has adapted to arid environments. It is usually rather nocturnal, except in reserves and other areas free from persecution. It feeds on a wide variety of animals and plants, including bees, honeycombs, termites, crops, berries and fruits and may also take sheep and cattle; many people are mauled and occasionally killed in encounters with them. Asiatic Black Bears grow to a maximum length of about 2 m and a weight of 150 kg; they are usually considerably smaller but occasionally larger – a weight of 173 kg is known. They mate in late autumn and the 2 or more cubs are born in late winter or early spring after a gestation of over 200 days, in a cave, hollow tree or thick cover. The cubs remain with the mother for 2 years or more and are sexually mature after about 3 years. Although not an endangered species, the Asiatic Black Bear has declined through extensive loss of habitat and the south Pakistan sub-species of Black Bear is classified as endangered. The Black Bear is commonly seen in zoos and frequently bred, sometimes through more than one generation. They have lived up to 33 years in captivity.

BROWN OR GRIZZLY BEAR *Ursus arctos*

The Brown Bear was at one time found over most of the northern hemisphere. It was once quite common, but with the spread of man's civilization is now rare or extinct over most of its former range. In the Old World it is found in the more remote parts of Europe (the Pyrenees, Abruzzi, the Italian Alps, Scandinavia and eastern Europe), and in Asia and the Middle East north of the Himalayas. In the New World, where it is usually known as the Grizzly it is found in western North America from Alaska and the Canadian north-west south to Mexico. However, the Mexican Grizzly is almost certainly extinct. Brown Bears are extremely variable – so much so that the New World animals, in particular, have often been considered a separate species. They vary in colour from a very pale

brown to dark brown or almost black and may have silvery hairs. A large European Brown Bear is about 1 m at the shoulder and weighs up to 265 kg, but the Kodiak Island Grizzly (the largest of the Brown Bears) may be up to 1.3 m at the shoulder and weigh 400 kg or more, but usually less. Brown Bears are omnivores eating a wide variety of berries, nuts, shoots and other plant matter, as well as small animals, carrion, insects, honey and occasionally domestic livestock. Usually 3, sometimes up to 6, tiny cubs (less than 500 g at birth) are born in the winter den, which they do not leave until about 4 months old. They become independent in their second summer. During the winter months Brown Bears hibernate for at least part of the time. They have been popular in zoos and menageries since ancient times, formerly being captured in Britain to take as far as Rome. They breed freely in captivity, and may live for up to 30 years; possibly as long as 50 years.

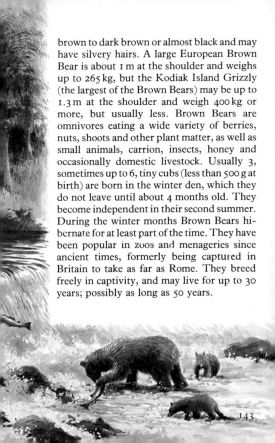

POLAR BEAR   *Thalarctos maritimus*

Polar Bears are found around the North Pole, in arctic Canada, Alaska, the USSR, Scandinavia and Greenland. They are almost marine in many parts of their range, living on ice floes and never coming to actual land. Unlike most other bears they do not have territories but wander continuously, even on floating icebergs. Although Polar Bears have been kept in menageries, circuses and zoos for many years, only in the last few decades have they been bred in captivity successfully. In Tudor times one kept in the Tower of London was allowed to catch fish in the Thames. At one time on the verge of extinction, but after many years strict protection now considered to be out of danger, Polar Bears are once more hunted in small numbers by eskimos. They are almost entirely carnivorous, feeding mainly on carrion, fish, seals and birds, but in summer take some lichens, mosses and berries. Females spend the winter in a den excavated in snow where 1 or 2 cubs are born after a gestation of about 240 days. Tiny at birth, weighing about 500 g, the cubs do not leave the den until about 4 months old, and do not become independent until their second year. Young Polar Bears are very playful, often gambolling in and around the water with their mother. When fully grown they are the largest of the bears, up to 2.5 m long, about 1.4 m at the shoulder and weighing up to 450 kg. They have lived for up to 33 years in captivity.

SUN BEAR *Helarctos malayanus*

The Sun Bear is found from Assam in the foothills of the Himalayas southwards through Bangladesh, Burma, Thailand and Malaya to Sumatra and Borneo. Sun Bears take their name from the mark on the chest which is whitish to dull orange and said to look like the rising sun. Sun Bears are mainly active at night, spending most of the day basking, usually several metres up in a tree, where they may break branches to make a crude nest.

Their feet all have 5 toes, with very powerful claws, which Sun Bears use for knocking down bees nests and tearing open termite mounds. Like other bears they eat a wide variety of plants and animals, but Sun Bears are particularly fond of honey and bee grubs and they can climb smooth, branchless trees easily, using only their claws which leave characteristic gouged marks. They also climb coconut palms to eat the growing point (palmite). Like other bears, Sun Bears exhibit considerable intelligence; a captive learned to turn the key in a locked cupboard, to get sugar, while another threw food around to attract chickens which it captured and ate. Sun Bears are the smallest and most lightly built of all the bears, growing to a length of about 1.4 m and a weight of up to 65 kg. They have short, rather coarse, black or brownish hair. The gestation period is about 95 days although up to 240 days have been recorded, when the development of the embryo is delayed; 1 or 2 cubs are born in each litter weighing about 325 gms. The cubbing den is often among the roots of a large forest tree. The young reach maturity at about 18 months and have lived for over 24 years in captivity. Like many other bears, the cubs of Sun Bears are frequently captured as pets, but as they mature they usually become increasingly dangerous. Many of the large zoos exhibit Sun Bears, but these are often pet animals that have grown up and eventually been sold or given away and they rarely breed successfully in captivity.

SLOTH BEAR *Melursus ursinus*

Sloth Bears are found in the forests of India, from the Himalayas and Assam south to Sri Lanka. They are mainly nocturnal and feed on a wide variety of animals and plants, including forest fruits such as banyans and other wild figs, mangoes, and various insects. As their name suggests, they move with a rather slow shuffle, though they are quite capable of short bursts of speed. They are also excellent climbers. They use their large and powerful claws to knock down or dig out termites which are one

of their main foods. As an aid to sucking termites out of their nests they have evolved a rather long snout with very mobile lips and their front incisors are missing. The snout is inserted and they then close their nostrils and suck in the termites. Near human settlements they also raid crops, such as sugar cane, and drink toddy from date palms where they are tapped. Although Sloth Bears are adaptable, and are still locally abundant, their habitat and range is increasingly being destroyed for farmland. The Sloth Bear is superficially similar to the Asiatic Black Bear, having black fur and a pale V-shaped mark on its chest, but at close quarters its elongated, pale snout and huge, pale, curved claws easily distinguish it. It grows to a length of up to 170 cm and males weigh up to 145 kg. After a gestation period of about 210 days, a litter of 1–3 cubs is born between early December and late January. At an early age the cubs are carried around by the mother, by clinging to the fur on her back. They are sexually mature at about 2–3 years. They are exhibited in many of the larger zoos, where they breed fairly regularly, although rarely for more than one generation. They have lived for up to 21 years in captivity.

COATIS

The Coatis or Coatimundis occur from the southern USA to Argentina. The Ring-tailed or Southern *Nasua nasua* and the White-nosed or Northern *N. narica* are the 2 species most often seen in zoos. Raccoon-like, but with rather short front legs, they grow to about 120 cm long, of which the tail (often held erect) is half, and weigh up to 12 kg. Diurnal and very active, they feed on small animals, birds, eggs and insects, as well as on a wide variety of fruit and vegetable matter. Bands of as many as 50 often feed together. The young are born hairless.

Ring-tailed Coati

CACOMISTLE   *Bassariscus astutus*

The Cacomistle or Ring-tailed Cat is rather Raccoon-like, but more slender. Of a total length of about 70 cm, the tail is 40 cm; it weighs only 5.5 kg. Cacomistles are widespread in the western and southern USA, southwards to southern Mexico. Like other members of the Raccoon family they are omnivores. Their preferred habitat is in rocky areas and chaparral, usually near water. A single litter of 3–4 young is born each year; the young leave the den at about 2 months and are independent after about 4 months. Cacomistles have lived for up to 8 years in captivity, but do not appear to have been bred very frequently in zoos.

A closely related species, *B. sumichrastri*, the Central American Cacomistle, is found from southern Mexico to Panama.

KINKAJOU *Potos flavus*

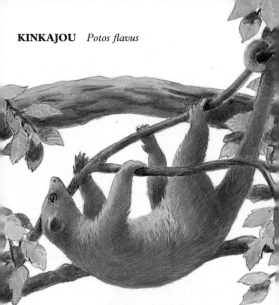

The Kinkajou is one of only 2 species of carnivores that have a prehensile tail (the other is the Binturong of south-east Asia, p. 189). It is found in the forests of Central and South America, from southern Mexico to the Mato Grosso. Its name derives from a native Indian name, as does its Latin name Potos, from another Indian name *Potto*. Curiously, in the forests of Africa, another quite unrelated, though superficially similar, animal has the native name of Potto (see p. 62). The Kinkajou has a head and body of up to 76 cm, a tail of up to 57 cm, and weighs up to 4.6 kg; males are larger than females. The Kinkajou is almost entirely arboreal and nocturnal, spending the daytime in a hollow tree, and emerging at night to feed among the upper branches of the forest. Although members of the carnivore family, Kinkajous are adapted to feeding mostly on fruit, although they do eat some insects as well as honey and even small vertebrates. They live alone or in pairs, or occasionally gather in small parties at a particular tree when laden with fruit. They have an exceptionally long tongue, used to extract the pulpy centres from fruit, which they often gather while suspended by their hind feet and tail, leaving the arms free. After a gestation of up to 118 days 1 or occasionally 2 helpless young are born in a nest in a hollow tree. Their eyes open at about 2 weeks and by 7 weeks they are taking solid food and can hang by their tails. Males are sexually mature at 18 months, females at 27 months. One has lived for over 23 years in captivity. Kinkajous can become very tame, and were often sold as 'honey bears' on account of their liking for honey. They are popular in zoos, and they breed quite regularly, through more than one generation.

Close relatives of the Kinkajou, are the 5 species of Olingo *Bassaricyon* spp., some of which are often found in the same areas as Kinkajous. They are little known and 2 of the species are only known from one locality each.

RACCOON *Procyon lotor*

Originally found only in North America, where it is widespread and often quite common, the Raccoon is now found living in the wild in parts of Europe and the USSR as a result of escapes from fur farms. The Raccoon grows to a length of about 1 m, of which the tail is approximately one-third, and weighs up to 15 kg. Raccoons are very active, and intelligent and very dexterous, using their forepaws as hands. Their German name of *Waschbär*, and French name of *Raton laveur*, as well the Latin *lotor*, all derive from their habit of washing their food. They are omnivores, but eat mainly animals, after hunting along rivers and streams where they find crustaceans, fish, molluscs and amphibians, as well as insects, birds and their eggs and small mammals; they also eat fruit and other plant matter and carrion. They make a den in a hollow tree, a rock cleft or even in the burrow of another animal, and a litter of usually 4 cubs is born in Spring; they may remain with the mother until the following spring but usually disperse in the autumn. Although Raccoons may lie up in their dens during the winter they do not actually hibernate. Raccoons are popular exhibits in zoos where they breed freely. They have also been captive-bred on a large scale by commercial fur farms. They have lived for 14 years in captivity. Raccoons often live close to man, scavenging in dustbins, and in many parts of North America they are often seen as road casualties.

There are another 6 closely related species of raccoons found in Central and South America; 5 of them are found only on islands and are little known and some may even be extinct. The sixth, the Crab-eating Raccoon *P. cancrivorus* is found from Costa Rica south to Peru and Uruguay, and is sometimes seen in zoos.

RED PANDA   *Ailurus fulgens*

The Red or Lesser Panda, or Cat Bear, together with the Giant Panda, is closely related to the raccoon family and more distantly to the bears. The Red Panda is superficially rather raccoon-like, in fact some scientists believe it to be a member of the raccoon family rather than the Pandas. Red Pandas are found in the Himalayas from Nepal and Sikkim eastwards to Burma and Szechuan in western China. They are found

mainly in temperate forests between 1500 m and spend most of the day asleep high in the trees, curled up like a cat with its tail over its head. Although a popular zoo animal, little is known of the Red Panda's biology in the wild. They are good climbers and feed mainly on plant matter, including berries, seeds and nuts, but occasionally eat birds' eggs, insects and grubs; in the wild they are active mainly at twilight and at night, descending to the ground around dusk to feed. The main threat to the Red Panda is the destruction of its habitat, and only a very small number are now left in India, but their popularity as a zoo animal led to an extensive trade in them. They tame easily, even when captured as adults, and in the past were sometimes kept as pets. The first Red Panda to be exhibited in a zoo arrived in London in 1869, since when they have been regularly seen in zoos throughout the world. They have been bred for more than one generation in several American and European zoos and are now bred in small numbers every year. When fully grown they are about 1 m long, of which the tail is just over one-third, and weigh up to 4.5 kg; they tend to look bigger and heavier on account of their long silky fur. In spring 1 or 2 young, occasionally 3 or 4, are born in a hollow tree after a gestation of 150 days. They stay with their parents until they are about 1 year old, or until the next litter is due. In captivity Red Pandas have lived for over 13 years.

GIANT PANDA
Ailuropoda melanoleuca

The Giant Panda has a very restricted distribution and is only found in a handful of remote mountainous bamboo forests in China. Its diet consists almost entirely of bamboo, although its bear-like teeth show that its ancestors were carnivores, and Pandas may still eat occasional small animals when they find them. At long intervals the bamboos flower and then die off; it is thought that this may be one of the causes of the Panda's rarity. In 1975–6, after the bamboo died, nearly 150 Pandas were found dead, and no doubt many more died without being found. The Giant Panda has been adopted as the symbol of the World Wildlife Fund and has come to symbolise rare and endangered species, just as the Dodo symbolises total extinction. In 1937 Chicago Zoo was the first to exhibit a Giant Panda (Su Lin), and ever since Pandas have remained the most popular (and valuable) of all zoo animals. By 1980, over 30 had been exhibited outside China, living for up to 14 years in captivity. In the 1970s several were presented by the Chinese Government to major zoos throughout the world. They have been bred in captivity in China for several years, and recently other zoos have been successful. The Giant Panda is one of the best-known and most distinctive mammals. It is generally bear-like in appearance and grows to nearly 2 m and a weight of up to 120 kg. It gives birth in winter to 2 tiny helpless young of which only one normally survives. Pandas do not become sexually mature until about 6 years old.

POLECATS

European Polecat

Marbled Polecat

Polecats are small carnivores closely related to the domestic ferret. The exact ancestry of the ferret is not known, but it is certainly closely related to both the Polecat *Mustela putorius* and the Steppe Polecat *M. eversmanni*, and it has been domesticated since at least the fourth century BC. Ferrets are normally creamy-white with pink eyes, but occasionally they are bred with markings like a pale Polecat and are then known as 'fitches'. The rarest ferret in the world is the Black-footed Ferret *M. nigripes* which lives in Prairie-dog cities on the borders of Canada and the USA, and was thought to be extinct until a few were rediscovered in 1981. The Polecat was formerly widespread over much of western and northern Europe but has declined due to persecution by gamekeepers, who claim it eats chickens and pheasants – its name is derived from the French *poule-chat* (chicken-cat). They were also known as *foulemarts* (as opposed to sweetmarts – pine martens) on account of their foul-smelling anal secretions. In recent years Polecats have started to recolonise parts of their former range in Britain. The Marbled Polecat *Vormela peregusa* is found in the steppes of eastern Europe and Asia, east to China. Both species feed mainly on mammals, particularly rodents and rabbits, and ground-nesting birds.

161

Domesticated Ferrets

STOAT AND WEASEL

Stoats and Weasels and their close relatives are among the smallest carnivores. One or more of them are found in nearly all parts of the world except for Australia (they have been introduced into New Zealand). For their size they are voracious predators, often tackling animals considerably larger than themselves. Both the Stoat *Musela erminea* and the Weasel *M. nivalis* are widespread in Europe, parts of Asia and North America. In the more northerly parts of their range both species turn white in winter, the Stoat retaining the black tip to its tail. This black tip is characteristic of ermine, used for trimming regalia and seen in heraldry. Weasels and Stoats are often persecuted for their alleged predation of game-birds, and they are also often hunted for their pelts, which are used in hundreds of thousands in the international fur trade. They feed on a wide variety of rodents, ground-birds, rabbits and other animals. Stoats have 1 litter per year of 5–6 kittens born after a gestation of about 2–12 months; Weasels have 2 litters of up to 10 kittens born after a gestation of only 35 days. Fully grown Stoats measure 40 cm, of which the tail is about one-quarter; Weasels grow to only 20 cm, plus a tail of 6 cm, but females are even smaller. Male Stoats eigh up to 300 g, Weasels up to 130 g. Several species of Weasel have been bred successfully in captivity and have been studied by biologists in laboratories.

Stoat

Stoat in winter (Ermine)

Stoat moulting

Weasel

MINK

European Mink

Mink are among the best known and most valuable fur bearing animals and consequently have been bred in captivity and a number of colour varieties developed. In the mid 1960s 22 million pelts were sold. They are not, however, very often exhibited in zoos. Wild American Mink *Mustela vison* are still extensively trapped for the fur trade and this species is the ancestor of the mink kept on fur farms. In the wild it is found in or near rivers and lakes throughout

Domesticated mink

Canada and much of the USA. It has also escaped from fur farms, or been deliberately introduced, in Britain and other parts of Europe, Iceland and the USSR. In many areas where it has been introduced it is now considered a pest. The European Mink *M. lutreola* is endangered in western and northern Europe, but is still widespread in eastern Europe through to Siberia. Both species grow to about 60 cm, of which the tail is just under one-third. On average European Mink are slightly smaller than American and often have more white on their lips. They are both found in mainly aquatic habitats where they are good swimmers and feed on a wide variety of small animals including frogs, voles, water-birds and fish. They give birth to up to 10 young (usually 2–7) after a gestation of about 50 days; the young open their eyes at about 25 days old.

European Mink

American Mink

MARTENS

American Marten

Pine Marten

Beech Marten

Martens are found in North America, Europe and Asia. There are 7 species, all fairly similar, of which the 3 illustrated are among the most widespread and familiar. All martens are valuable as furbearers – the pelt of the Sable, *Martes zibellina*, found in the Soviet Union, is one of the most valuable in the world – and they have been hunted extensively. In many parts of their range they have been exterminated but although they are still rare in many areas, none are believed to be endangered; in fact under protection and with reintroduction programmes they are once more extending their range. Martens are often seen in zoos and are occasionally bred in captivity. The American Marten *M. americana* which grows to a maximum of about 65 cm, including a tail of 15 cm, is found in wooded areas of Canada and the northern USA. The Pine Marten *M. martes* grows to about 75 cm, of which the tail is about one-third, and is found in most of Europe, except for Spain and the Balkans, east to Siberia. The Beech Marten *M. foina*, roughly the same size as the Pine Marten, but more heavily built, lives in most of Europe, except for Britain and northern Scandinavia, and through western Asia as far as the Himalayas. Martens are agile, often climbing trees, and feed on birds, squirrels and other animals. The females in all martens are smaller than males. In spring, 2–6 kittens are born; they are very small and their eyes open at about 5–6 weeks. All three species have lived 17 years in captivity.

ZORILLA *Ictonyx striatus*

The Zorilla or Striped Polecat is the African equivalent of the skunks of the Americas (p. 177). It grows to a total length of about 60 cm of which the tail is less than half; it weighs up to 1.5 kg, males being heavier than females. The Zorilla is found in open country over most of Africa south of the Sahara, but not in dense forest. It feeds on birds, reptiles, mammals and invertebrates up to the size of a hare, which it hunts mainly in twilight or at night. Although they are mostly terrestrial they can climb and swim well. The 1–3 young are born after a gestation of about 36 days in a burrow, among crevices or even in barns or other buildings. They are helpless for a comparatively long period, taking their first solid food after a month and opening their eyes at about 6 weeks; they are weaned at 18 weeks and independent at 20 weeks. They are completely solitary and will not even tolerate the opposite sex. In addition to a superficial similarity in appearance to American skunks, Zorillas have similar behaviour. When alarmed by an intruder or predator they erect the fur on their back and stiffly raise the tail, before ejecting a foul-smelling fluid from the anal gland. They also emit a high-pitched scream when alarmed, and if attacked by a large predator sometimes sham death. Zorillas are closely related to the Saharan Striped Weasel (*Poecilictis libyca*) and White-naped Weasel (*Poecilogale albinucha*) which also have skunk-like markings. The Zorilla is comparatively rare in zoos, but has been bred and has lived over 13 years in captivity.

WOLVERINE *Gulo gulo*

The Wolverine or Glutton, the largest member of the
weasel family, was originally found throughout the
more northerly parts of Europe, Asia and America,
but is now extinct or rare in many parts of this range.
Wolverines have been trapped for their fur, which
was often used to line and edge parka hoods, as it does
not trap water and so ice from condensed breath can
easily be brushed off, unlike most other furs which
become encrusted or soggy. Wolverines are found
mainly in open tundra; although formerly they also
occurred in forested areas they are now rare in this
habitat. They eat a wide variety of animals and plants
and have a reputation as a fierce and greedy predator.
They scent-mark uneaten food with strong smelling
secretions. Wolverines are rather ungainly, but can
move very fast over short distances, and their broad
feet enable them to chase reindeer and other animals

over snow. They are normally solitary, with large territories which may occasionally overlap. After a gestation of 60–120 days, but sometimes much longer, 2–4 young are born in an underground den in late winter. When fully grown they are about 1 m long, plus a tail of about 20 cm, and weigh about 15 kg. American animals are, however, on average larger than those from the Old World, and all gain weight before hibernation. Wolverines are occasionally kept in zoos but rarely breed. They have been known to live for over 17 years in captivity. In addition to being hunted for their pelts they are often persecuted because they are alleged to kill Reindeer (Caribou) and devour animals caught in leg-hold traps.

HONEY BADGER *Mellivora capensis*

The Honey Badger or Ratel is widespread over most of Africa south of the Sahara and eastwards through Arabia to India. It is found in a wide range of habitats, from tropical moist forest to deserts, and where undisturbed may be active by day as well as by night. The most remarkable feature of the Honey Badger is its association with a bird – the Honey Guide *Indicator indicator*. This leads the Honey Badger to wild bees' nests, which the badger rips open to obtain the honey and the bee grubs, exposing also the wax of the combs on which the Honey Guide feeds. In addition to honey, the diet

includes a wide variety of animals up to the size of small antelope, and also snakes (including poisonous ones such as mambas). Honey Badgers can be very dangerous when cornered and will even attack animals as large as Buffalo; they have extremely powerful jaws. Their dens are in hollow trees, rock crevices, or excavated in the ground, where 1–2 young are born after a gestation of about 180 days. Young animals are rusty brown above and lack the contrasting pale band of the adults. When fully grown they are about the same size and weight as the badgers of Europe and America. Honey Badgers are comparatively rare in zoos, but have lived for 24 years in captivity.

Greater Honey Guide

BADGERS

Eurasian Badger

The Eurasian Badger *Meles meles* is widely distributed over most of Europe, across Asia to Japan. Although it has now disappeared from much of its former range, it is still surprisingly abundant in some areas. Badgers are mostly nocturnal and live in extensive burrows known as setts; because of their nocturnal habits they are rarely kept in zoos. Two or 3 young are born in early spring after a gestation of about 65 days or more. They emerge from the sett at 6 weeks old, grow to 1 m long and are mature at 2 years. They have lived for 16 years in captivity.

The American Badger *Taxidea taxus* is similar in appearance to the Eurasian Badger, and is widespread in North America from California and central Mexico north to central Canada. Like the Eurasian Badger, it is mainly nocturnal and in the wild is most likely to be seen along highways at dusk or dawn. It digs extensive burrows and also digs in search of rodents, which are its main prey. Two to 5 young are born in early spring, and when fully grown are about 80 cm long and weigh up to 10 kg. Although they eat large numbers of rodents, American Badgers are often persecuted because of their burrowing; in the past they have also been hunted for their pelts. They are rarely seen in zoos outside North America, but they have lived for up to 12 years in captivity.

American Badger

STRIPED SKUNK *Mephitis mephitis*

One of the best known mammals in North America, the Striped Skunk is often seen (and smelled) dead on highways. It is famous for its ability to spray an evil-smelling fluid from an anal gland, over a distance of 5 or 6 m; this is used to deter predators and, apart from its foul smell, temporarily blinds the intruder. The Striped Skunk is found from Canada southwards through the USA to northern Mexico. It grows to over 75 cm including a tail of up to 40 cm, and weighs up to 2 kg; males are larger than females. It is mainly nocturnal and is omnivorous, feeding on a wide variety of animals and plants including mice, insects, berries, fruit and carrion. It makes its den in burrows, hollow logs, in rock piles, and under buildings, where the females bears up to 10 young (usually 5 or 6) after a gestation of up to 63 days. In the northern parts of its range Striped Skunks sleep for days on end in cold weather, but do not go into true hibernation. When they leave the nest the young follow the mother in single file. Although large numbers of Striped Skunks are killed on roads, and in the past have been hunted for their skins, they are still abundant over most of their range. The Striped Skunk is the species most commonly seen in zoos, where it is occasionally bred and has lived for 13 years.

There are a number of related species, including the Hooded Skunk *M. macroura*, 4 species of spotted skunks *Spilogale* spp and 7 species of hog-nosed skunks *Conepatus* spp. All are confined to the New World.

EURASIAN OTTER   *Lutra lutra*

The Eurasian Otter was once widespread throughout Europe, North Africa and Asia as far south as Java and Sumatra. In most of western Europe, however, except for Scotland, Ireland and parts of Scandinavia, and some other parts of their range, otters are now extinct or are very rare. They live in aquatic habitats, including rivers, lakes, estuaries and sea coasts, and eat a wide variety of fish, particularly eels, as well as rodents, frogs, birds, crustaceans and even carrion. The Eurasian Otter grows to about 130 cm including the tail, which is about one-third of the total length, and weighs up to about 15 kg.

The closely related American River Otter *L. canadensis* is almost identical in appearance and behaviour and is widespread in the Americas. It is often exhibited in zoos.

Up to 5 cubs (usually 2 or 3) are born at any time of the year after a gestation of about 60 days in a burrow (holt), usually close to water. The cubs are blind at birth and open their eyes at about 4 weeks; they leave the nest at about 6 weeks and are independent at 6–9 months. Otters are very playful, even when adult, making slides on river banks and tobogganing in snow. Although they are often kept in zoos, the Eurasian Otter rarely breeds in captivity; however, experimental reintroduction programmes of captive-bred and hand-reared otters have been started. The Otter Trust in England has specialised in breeding European Otters.

ASIATIC SMALL-CLAWED OTTER
Aonyx cinerea

The Asiatic Small-clawed or Clawless Otter is found in and close to rivers, streams, reservoirs, lakes, rice paddies and estuaries over much of India and Southeast Asia, from the foothills of the Himalayas east through Assam, Bengal and Burma, to southern China in the east, and the Malay Peninsula, Borneo, Java and the Philippines in the south. As its name suggests it has only rudimentary claws. It is a small species, growing to a maximum of 55 cm plus a tail of up to 35 cm; it weighs up to 6 kg. The Asiatic Small-clawed Otter feeds on a wide variety of animals, but possibly takes less fish than most other otters and more crabs, molluscs and other small animals. Little is known about it in the wild but, because it does little damage to fisheries, is not particularly valued for its pelt, and has adapted to living close to man, it is probably only threatened by habitat destruction and pollution. Asiatic Small-clawed Otters are one of the most popular species of otter in zoos, usually becoming very tame as well as being active and playful. They are regularly bred in small numbers with litters of 4–6 commonly recorded, and they have been bred for more than one generation.

Closely related are 2 African species: the African Clawless Otter *A. capensis* which is widespread over much of Africa south of the Sahara, and occasionally exhibited in zoos, and the Zaire Clawless Otter *A. congica* which is found in the basin of the Zaire River.

LINSANG

The African Linsang *Poiana richardsoni* is found in separated areas in West and Central Africa – from Sierra Leone to Zaire, and also on the island of Fernando Po. They are confined to rain forest where they are entirely nocturnal and generally arboreal and feed on a variety of small animals including insects, birds and lizards, and also fruit. They build nests in which to sleep, and give birth to 2 or 3 young. The African Linsang is genet-like in appearance, but with a proportionally longer tail, growing to a length of up to 38 cm plus a tail of up to 40 cm, weighing up to 700 gms.

There are two other species of Linsang found in

Spotted Linsang

Asia; the Banded Linsang *Prionodon linsang* found from Thailand south to Java and Borneo, and the Spotted Linsang *Prionodon pardicolor* which is widespread from Nepal, eastwards to Indo-china. The Spotted Linsang is very similar in size and appearance to the African Linsang, and the Banded has the markings of the back joined into broad bands. In habit they are very similar to the African species. Because they are all found primarily in mature forest it is likely that their range is decreasing. Although they adapt readily to captivity, they are not often seen in zoos, and only rarely breed in captivity. A Banded Linsang has lived over 8 years in captivity.

Banded Linsang

GENETS

Large-spotted Genet

The Large-spotted or Rusty-spotted Genet *Genetta tigrina* is widespread over most of Africa south of the Sahara, except in dry and arid areas. The preferred habitats include forest edges and clearings, bush country, agricultural lands and, in particular, wet, swampy areas such as reed beds and thickets. It grows to a length of up to 55 cm, plus a tail only slightly shorter, standing about 18 cm at the shoulder and weighing up to about 3 kg. There is considerable variation in the coloration and patterning, and very dark, melanistic animals are common. Genets are mainly active at dusk and at night, hiding by day in hollow trees, or among rocks or in burrows. They prey on a wide variety of small animals up to the size of Guinea fowl or Hare, and may take domestic poultry. Little is recorded of the biology of the Large-spotted Genet, but there are probably up to 4 young, which are dark grey at birth. They develop the adult pattern by about 6 weeks, and are weaned at 2–3 months. The Large-spotted Genet is the species most commonly seen in zoos and has lived for up to $9\frac{1}{2}$ years in captivity. It is closely related to others, several of which are exhibited occasionally.

The Small-spotted or Common Genet *G. genetta*, which occurs in south-west Europe, as well as in Africa and Arabia, was frequently tamed in Ancient Egypt, and kept as a pet to hunt rats and mice. Common Genets give birth to 1–4 young after a gestation of 56–77 days and become sexually mature at about 4 years. They have lived for 13 years in captivity. There are 9 other closely related genets found in Africa, all of which are only rarely seen in zoos. They have been hunted for their furs, and in recent years with the decline of several species of spotted cats, genet fur has become involved in international trade.

CIVETS

There are over 20 species of civets, which are closely related to the genets and mongooses. The African Palm Civet *Nandina binotata* occurs in forest areas, from Guinea and the southern Sudan, south to Zimbabwe and Angola, where it is largely arboreal and nocturnal. They grow to a length of up to 58 cm plus a tail of up to 62 cm and weigh about 2 kg. Up to 4 young (usually 1 or 2) are born after a gestation of 64 days. The young are sexually mature in their third year, and they have lived 16 years in captivity. One of the best known is the Common Palm Civet or Toddy

Common Palm Civet

Cat *Paradoxurus hermaphroditus* which is found in southern and south-east Asia and is most abundant in well-wooded areas, where they hide up in hollow trees or lie along branches by day and emerge to hunt at night. But they are very adaptable and are often found in mango or palm plantations and even live in the centre of big cities, where they feed extensively on rats and mice and occasionally raid poultry. They also eat a large amount of fruit, and where palm trees are tapped they climb to drink the juice (toddy) which collects over night. It is often exhibited in zoos, where it breeds regularly and has lived for up to 22 years. Other civets are also occasionally exhibited, including the African Civet which is exploited for its musk glands. Madagascar is the home of several unusual civets and their relatives, some of which are occasionally seen in zoos.

Palm Civets eat a wide range of foods

BINTURONG *Arctictis binturong*

In general appearance the Binturong or Bear-cat is much more bear-like than the other civets, to which it is closely related. It is the only Old World mammal to have a properly developed prehensile tail. It is found from Nepal and Bhutan eastwards through Bangladesh, Burma and south to the Malay Peninsula, Borneo, Java and Palawan. Although Binturongs are widespread, they are nowhere common. They live almost exclusively in dense forest where they are nocturnal and mainly arboreal. They are good climbers and use the tip of their prehensile tail when clambering about, particularly when descending trees; they also swim and dive, but rarely leap. They are omnivorous feeders taking fruit, small animals, leaves, berries and eggs. The Binturong's colouring is very variable, though generally blackish. Some individuals may have white and buff hairs, on occasion so many as to make them appear greyish. They grow to about 95 cm, plus a tail of 90 cm, and weigh up to 14 kg. Up to 6, but usually 2, young are born after a gestation of about 3 months, and reach adult size at about 1 year old. The female may have two litters a year. Binturongs are very vocal with a wide range of hisses, growls and grunts. The only serious threat to the Binturong in the wild is probably that of habitat loss. Despite being quite fierce when captured, Binturongs easily tame if taken when young and are commonly kept in most of the world's zoos, where they are frequently bred. The longest recorded captive lifespan is over 22 years.

MEERCAT *Suricata suricatta*

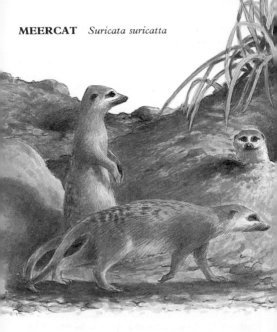

The Meercat or Suricate is a polecat-sized mongoose
confined to South Africa and Angola, where it is one
of the characteristic animals of the open country.
Meercats live in colonies of up to 30, often associating
with ground squirrels and Yellow Mongooses. When

feeding, in pairs or small groups, they often rest on their haunches to keep watch for intruders, which led the early Dutch settlers to compare their appearance with that of ninepins. When alarmed they stand on tip-toe, using their tail for support and craning their neck to see the cause of alarm, before scampering underground. Meercats are active by day and feed in an area of up to 200 m around their burrows. They spend the early morning sunbathing near the burrow entrance and the rest of the day searching restlessly for food, which includes a few small mammals, lizards and birds, but mainly consists of insects, spiders and other invertebrates, together with roots, bulbs, tubers, shoots, fruit and other vegetable matter. Probably because they feed almost exclusively around their burrows, Meercats migrate when they have exhausted the food supply and may occupy different warrens a mile or more apart. As they are active, sociable animals, Meercats are popular exhibits in many zoos and often breed freely. They have lived for over 8 years in captivity. In the wild they breed at all times of the year, but the main breeding season is from October to April, and up to 5 young (usually 2–3) are born after a gestation of 77 days. The young are weaned at 4–6 weeks, independent at 10 weeks and sexually mature at 9 months. When fully grown they are about 30 cm long, plus a tail of 24 cm, and weigh up to 1 kg. Their enemies include jackals, wild cats, Honey Badgers and many birds of prey.

EGYPTIAN MONGOOSE
Herpestes ichneumon

The Egyptian Mongoose or Ichneumon is widespread in Africa and occurs in a great variety of habitats, except for the deserts of the Sahara and south-west Africa. It is also found in southern Europe. This species together with several other of 15 *Herpestes* mongooses, is sometimes seen in zoos. The best known is probably the Indian Grey Mongoose *H. edwardsi*, immortalised as Riki-Tiki-Tavi by Rudyard Kipling, and to be seen captive in many street snake-and-mongoose fights in India and the Far East. Mongooses are mainly active by day and sleep in a burrow, hollow log or rock crevice. They feed on a wide variety of rodents, birds and their eggs, reptiles, amphibians and crustaceans, and are able to kill poisonous snakes because they move fast, with the added protection of coarse fur around the neck to deflect bites. After a gestation of 49–77 days up to 4 (usually 3) young are born. Both parents help to rear the young. When fully grown, at 1 year, they are nearly 1 m long, of which the tail is about one-third, and weigh up to 4 kg. They are sexually mature at 2 years old.

AARDWOLF *Proteles cristatus*

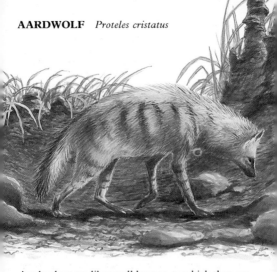

Aardwolves are like small hyenas, to which they are related, and take their name from the Afrikaans for earth, because of their burrowing habits. They are found from eastern to southern Africa; although their range extends from the north-eastern Sudan to the Cape Province of South Africa, and to the Central African Republic, their distribution is patchy and very poorly known in many places. They are found mainly in dry, open country and they mark a territory of about 1.5 km around their burrow by leaving secretions from the anal gland; they also have large defecating sites to mark their territory and can eject scent from their anal gland when attacked. Aardwolves are active at dusk and by night and are almost exclusively insectivorous, feeding on termites, which they rapidly lick up from the ground. In captivity they have fed on other animals including birds, but there is no evidence they do so in the wild. They are normally solitary, except in the breeding season, when the male helps to rear the young; occasionally 2 families may share a burrow. There are 1–5 cubs in a litter which are born after a gestation of up to 110 days, and after weaning the young are fed by the parents on regurgitated termites. When fully grown they are about 80 cm long, plus a tail of about 30 cm, and stand about 50 cm at the shoulder; they weigh up to 14 kg. The long crest-like hair on the back gave rise to its Afrikaans name of 'manhaarjakkal' = maned jackal. Although Aardwolves have lived for over 14 years in captivity, they are not often exhibited in zoos and have only rarely been bred.

HYENAS

Brown Hyena

Striped Hyena

Spotted Hyena

The 3 species of hyenas are closely related to the Aardwolf. The Brown Hyena *Hyaena brunnea* grows to a length of up to 1.25 m, height of 80 cm and weight of 55 kg. It is the rarest and least widely distributed, being restricted to southern Africa south of a line approximately from south Angola to the Zambesi in Mozambique. The Striped Hyena *H. hyaena* grows to a length of up to 1.2 m and height of 80 cm, and weighs 45 kg; the male is slightly larger than the female. It was once widespread over the northern half of Africa, through Asia Minor, the Middle East and southern Asia to India. The Spotted Hyena *Crocuta crocuta* grows to a length of up to 1.8 m and height of 90 cm, and weighs up to 85 kg; females are larger than males. It is widespread in most of the more open habitats in Africa south of the Sahara. Once thought to be scavengers, hyenas are now known to be powerful predators whose kills lions often scavenge. They take a wide variety of animal prey, as well as carrion and fruit, and even raid badly buried human remains. They are able to crush and eat bones, making their droppings a characteristic chalky-white. Spotted and Striped Hyenas are the species most frequently seen in zoos, where both breed occasionally. The Striped Hyena is usually solitary, except during the breeding season when it lives in pairs and the male helps to rear the 2–4 young. The Spotted Hyena is much more sociable, usually living in pairs or small groups, and occasionally in troops of 100 or more. Striped Hyenas have lived for up to 24 years in captivity, Spotted Hyenas for up to 40 years.

European Lynx

Bobcat

Caracal

LYNX, BOBCAT AND CARACAL

Between them these medium-sized, closely related, short-tailed cats are (or were) found over most of North America, Europe, Asia and Africa. The Lynx *Felis lynx*, the most northerly species, found mainly in well-wooded habitats in Europe, Asia, the northern USA and Canada and once widespread in the woodlands of Europe, is now reduced to isolated populations. One of the more heavily spotted forms, the Pardel Lynx, found in south-west Spain and Portugal, is endangered. The Bobcat *F. rufus* is found from southern Canada through the USA to Mexico, and the Caracal *F. caracal* over most of Africa, Asia Minor, Arabia, the southern USSR and east to central India. The Lynx grows to about 130 cm plus a tail of 25 cm, the Bobcat to about 75 cm plus a tail of 23 cm and the Caracal to 90 cm, plus a tail of 30 cm and a weight of 8 kg. They all feed on a wide variety of birds and mammals, and the Caracal has even been trained in India and Iran to hunt hares and game-birds. A litter of 2–3 kittens is born after a gestation of 50–60 days. They mature at about 1 year and may breed the following year. Lynx and Bobcat are extensively exploited for the fur trade, particularly in Canada and the USA where they are extinct in many parts of their ranges. All are exhibited in zoos and breed fairly regularly in captivity, where Lynx have lived for up to 18 years, Caracals 17 years and Bobcats 25 years. Captive-bred Lynx have been successfully re-introduced into the wild.

PUMA *Felis concolor*

The Puma, Mountain Lion or Cougar was formerly found almost the length and breadth of the Americas, and despite relentless persecution still has a fairly wide range in western and southern North America, and in Central and South America. It is now mainly found in mountainous areas, where it may occupy territories of up to 650 km². The Puma is nearly as large as the Jaguar, growing up to 275 cm, including a tail of 90 cm, and weighing 100 kg; but there is considerable variation in both size and colour. Outside the breeding season pumas are usually solitary and take virtually any prey from insects to horses. Their preferred prey, however, is deer (in North America), which the Puma stalks rather like a domestic cat. When it has finished eating, it hides the remains of its prey under leaves and other vegetation. Up to 6 (usually 2–4) spotty kittens are born after a gestation of about 96 days. They are weaned at 6 weeks and reared by the female alone, and become independent at about 1 year. Pumas are seen in almost all large zoos and breed freely in captivity.

OCELOT AND MARGAY

Ocelot

The Ocelot *Felis pardalis* and the similar, smaller Tree Ocelot or Margay *Felis weidi* are both widely distributed in the forests of South and Central America. Very little is known about them in the wild, although hundreds of thousands have been killed for the fur trade and large numbers of young Ocelots and

Margays were once imported into the USA as pets. The Ocelot occurs as far north as the southern states of the USA, but almost everywhere it is becoming rare and many populations are now endangered. It is diurnal, but has become nocturnal in areas close to man, and preys on small mammals up to the size of a young peccary in a territory which it marks with scent. During the breeding season it catawauls like a domestic cat, but louder. The Ocelot grows to a length of about 100 cm plus a tail of up to 45 cm, and the Margay, to about 80 cm plus a tail of 50 cm. In both species the colour and pattern are rather variable. Several other species of cats also occur in South America, but are rarely seen in zoos.

Margay

SERVAL *Felis serval*

The Serval is a medium-sized, rather long legged cat, growing to about 90 cm, plus a tail of up to 35 cm, and weighing up to 15 kg. It is found in Africa and is widely distributed in fairly open country, up to 3000 m, south of the Sahara, with an isolated population in North Africa. Servals are mainly found in savannahs and open woodlands, but usually near water and with abundant thick cover. Their markings are very variable and black forms occur. Servals are solitary and extremely agile hunters, taking a wide variety of prey ranging from mice and other rodents to small antelope, and also birds up to the size of guineafowl which are often captured with a leap into the air. After a gestation of up to 77 days, 1–4 (usually 2–3) kittens are born in a den, usually in a burrow under rocks or in a thicket; they are weaned at about 6 months, independent at the end of their first year and sexually mature at 2 years. In recent years Servals have been heavily exploited by the fur trade. In zoos they breed fairly readily, and have lived for over 17 years in captivity.

Prey of Servals includes Mole Rats (left) and Chestnut-bellied Sandgrouse (below)

WILD CAT *Felis silvestris*

Wild cats grow to about 130 cm, of which the tail is about one-third, and weigh a maximum of 15 kg, but are usually 5–10 kg. The Wild Cat is the ancestor of the domestic cat and in Europe is often similar to a rather large tabby cat with a thickly furred tail,

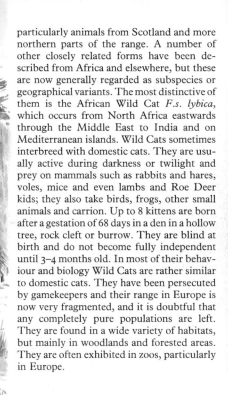

particularly animals from Scotland and more northern parts of the range. A number of other closely related forms have been described from Africa and elsewhere, but these are now generally regarded as subspecies or geographical variants. The most distinctive of them is the African Wild Cat *F.s. lybica*, which occurs from North Africa eastwards through the Middle East to India and on Mediterranean islands. Wild Cats sometimes interbreed with domestic cats. They are usually active during darkness or twilight and prey on mammals such as rabbits and hares, voles, mice and even lambs and Roe Deer kids; they also take birds, frogs, other small animals and carrion. Up to 8 kittens are born after a gestation of 68 days in a den in a hollow tree, rock cleft or burrow. They are blind at birth and do not become fully independent until 3–4 months old. In most of their behaviour and biology Wild Cats are rather similar to domestic cats. They have been persecuted by gamekeepers and their range in Europe is now very fragmented, and it is doubtful that any completely pure populations are left. They are found in a wide variety of habitats, but mainly in woodlands and forested areas. They are often exhibited in zoos, particularly in Europe.

LION *Panthera leo*

African Lion and Lioness

Male Lions grow to about 2 m, plus a tail of 1 m, and weigh up to 200 kg; they are markedly bigger than females and normally have impressive manes. The Lion was once found throughout the more open parts of Africa and south-east Europe, and east through

Asia Minor and Arabia to India. It is now extinct in the northern parts of its range, except for an isolated population in the forest of Gir in India; it survived in the Middle East until well into this century. They are often vocal, and the male's roar can be heard by humans up to 9 km away. Lions generally seem lazy, but hunt by day or night, usually in groups (prides), preying on a wide variety of large mammals and also scavenging. They hunt by stalking their prey, and by making a final charge, suffocating or strangling large prey and killing small animals with a swipe from their paw. After gestation of up to 113 days a litter of 1–4 (usually 2–3) cubs is born in a den in a thicket among rocks. The cubs are spotted at birth and weaned at 6 months, but are not sexually mature until 18 months and fully grown until 5 or 6 years. Lions breed prolifically in captivity, where they have lived for up to 30 years, and there is a considerable annual surplus of captive-bred animals.

Asiatic Lion

JAGUAR *Panthera onca*

The largest cat in the New World, in the wild the Jaguar normally grows to 270 cm, plus a tail of 75 cm, and weighs up to 100 kg. Its colour is variable, but generally tawny with black spots which form rosettes. Completely black Jaguars also commonly occur. The Jaguar was once found in the Southern USA and throughout most of Central and South America, but habitat destruction and hunting have exterminated it over a very large part of its range and it is now a threatened species. It is an excellent swimmer and climber. Females are believed to breed in alternate years and 1–4 (usually 2) cubs are born after a gestation of about 100 days. The cubs are not independent until 2 years old. Jaguars feed on a variety of mainly mammal prey, including peccaries, deer, tapir, and capybara, and also on large birds, small caimans and freshwater turtles; they occasionally take domestic animals. They are commonly kept in most larger zoos and black Jaguars are often exhibited. They breed freely in captivity. When the conquistadors discovered Mexico City the Aztecs had a large zoo which included Jaguars – allegedly fed upon human flesh.

LEOPARD *Panthera pardus*

The Leopard was once widespread over almost the entire continent of Africa, and also throughout southern Asia from Turkey to eastern China and south to the Malay archipelago and Sri Lanka. Its markings are vari-

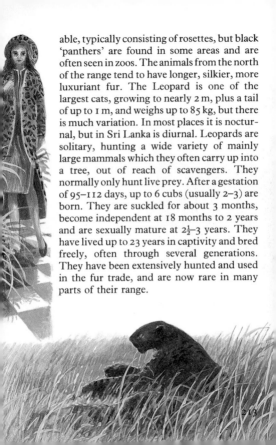

able, typically consisting of rosettes, but black 'panthers' are found in some areas and are often seen in zoos. The animals from the north of the range tend to have longer, silkier, more luxuriant fur. The Leopard is one of the largest cats, growing to nearly 2 m, plus a tail of up to 1 m, and weighs up to 85 kg, but there is much variation. In most places it is nocturnal, but in Sri Lanka is diurnal. Leopards are solitary, hunting a wide variety of mainly large mammals which they often carry up into a tree, out of reach of scavengers. They normally only hunt live prey. After a gestation of 95–112 days, up to 6 cubs (usually 2–3) are born. They are suckled for about 3 months, become independent at 18 months to 2 years and are sexually mature at 2½–3 years. They have lived up to 23 years in captivity and bred freely, often through several generations. They have been extensively hunted and used in the fur trade, and are now rare in many parts of their range.

TIGER *Panthera tigris*

Siberian Tiger

The tiger is the largest of the cats, growing to a maximum of about 3 m of which the tail is just over one-third. There is, however, enormous variation in size – those from Siberia being the largest and those from Indonesia the smallest. Tigers once ranged from Asia Minor and the Middle East, across the southern USSR and India to Korea and Manchuria in the east, and south to Bali, Sumatra and Java. Now, remnant populations are confined to India, Siberia, and south through Indo-China to the Malay archipelago. Its numbers are also a fraction of former times. The decline is largely due to persecution, particularly in the colonial period, when thousands were killed annually until the 1950s. Tigers are usually solitary and, due to persecution, nocturnal. After a gestation of 105–113 days up to 6 (usually 1–4) kittens are born. They are weaned at about 11 weeks and are sexually mature in their fourth year. Tigers are one of the most popular exhibits in zoos and they breed freely – some females have produced over 30 cubs. They have lived for 26 years in captivity.

Bengal Tiger

SNOW LEOPARD *Panthera uncia*

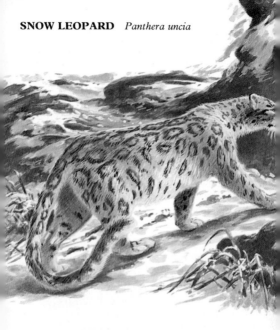

The Snow Leopard or Ounce is a large, thick-furred cat, growing up to 110 cm with a thickly furred tail of 90 cm. The winter fur is over 6 cm long on the back and even longer on the belly. Snow Leopards are found in the Himalayas from Kashmir to Bhutan and northwards into Tibet, central Asia and the Altai, often living above the tree line, some 3400 m above sea level, and occasionally at over 5000 m. They are hardly ever seen in the wild and little studied. They are mainly nocturnal hunters, preying on wild sheep and goats, musk deer, hares and marmots and other rodents and birds. Some individuals habitually prey on domestic stock. Nothing is known of their breeding in the wild; in captivity, there are usually 2 kittens in a litter which is born after a gestation of 93 days. Many of the major zoos of the world keep Snow Leopards and they are now breeding fairly freely. The only other cat found in the bleak mountains of the Himalayas is Pallas' Cat or Manul *Felis manul*, rare in zoos, which, like the Snow Leopard, is a threatened species.

CLOUDED LEOPARD
Neofelis nebulosa

The Clouded Leopard is found in forested country in the Himalayas, eastwards to Assam and southern China and Taiwan, and southwards through the Malay Peninsula to Sumatra and Borneo; throughout its range it is rather sparsely distributed, and probably nowhere common. It is normally nocturnal and

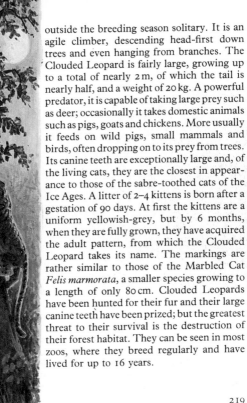

outside the breeding season solitary. It is an agile climber, descending head-first down trees and even hanging from branches. The Clouded Leopard is fairly large, growing up to a total of nearly 2 m, of which the tail is nearly half, and a weight of 20 kg. A powerful predator, it is capable of taking large prey such as deer; occasionally it takes domestic animals such as pigs, goats and chickens. More usually it feeds on wild pigs, small mammals and birds, often dropping on to its prey from trees. Its canine teeth are exceptionally large and, of the living cats, they are the closest in appearance to those of the sabre-toothed cats of the Ice Ages. A litter of 2–4 kittens is born after a gestation of 90 days. At first the kittens are a uniform yellowish-grey, but by 6 months, when they are fully grown, they have acquired the adult pattern, from which the Clouded Leopard takes its name. The markings are rather similar to those of the Marbled Cat *Felis marmorata*, a smaller species growing to a length of only 80 cm. Clouded Leopards have been hunted for their fur and their large canine teeth have been prized; but the greatest threat to their survival is the destruction of their forest habitat. They can be seen in most zoos, where they breed regularly and have lived for up to 16 years.

CHEETAH *Acinonyx jubatus*

The Cheetah is a large, long-legged cat with a short, rather small head. It grows to a length of up to 140 cm plus a tail of 80 cm, and weighs up to 60 kg; females are slightly smaller than males. Cheetahs were formerly widespread and occurred in most of the more open habitats in Africa, and also north and east through the Middle East to India. Now they are only found in a small area in Iran and the USSR and in Africa south of the Sahara, where they are mostly declining or very rare. They hunt by day and feed mainly on mammals, which they run down at speeds of up to 110 kpt (69 mph) – the fastest land mammal. They usually knock their prey over, then seize it by the throat and strangle it; most hunts are unsuccessful, and consequently disturbance by humans can have a very harmful effect. Their preferred prey is usually gazelles, such as impalas, and the calves of larger antelope. Cheetahs live singly, in pairs or in small family groups, but usually hunt alone. After a gestation of about 95 days up to 6 (usually 2–4) kittens are born, which are weaned by 3–6 months and independent at about 18 months. Cheetahs are fairly vocal; they purr in contentment, they also have a loud yelp that can be heard by humans 2 km away. In the past Cheetahs were frequently tamed and kept for hunting gazelles and antelope in India and other parts of Asia; the use of wild-caught Cheetahs in this way goes back at least 4300 years, and they were imported into Europe during the Renaissance. Nowadays they are to be seen in most zoos and safari parks, but it is only recently (since 1960) that they have been successfully bred and even now only a few zoos are breeding them. They have lived for up to 19 years in captivity.

CALIFORNIAN SEA-LION
Zalophus californianus

The Californian Sea-lion is found along the Pacific coast of North America, and on the Galapagos Islands; it formerly occurred in Japanese waters but this population is now probably extinct. Californian Sea-lions are frequently seen in zoos and also as performing animals in circuses. They have good memories and once tamed will perform tricks even after a gap of several months. They were once extensively hunted for their skins or for oil for their blubber. They are relatively small, males growing to about 2.5 m and the females to 1.8 m, and a weight of up to 300 and 100 kg respectively. They have large eyes, small pointed ears, and flippers which can be turned forwards, allowing them to gallop on land (unlike true seals). They are fast swimmers, at up to 20 knots, and often 'porpoise', females can jump up to 2 m clear of the water. After a gestation of about 340 days they produce a single pup, and they breed freely in captivity. Some have been released in the Mediterranean from time to time, where they may still live ferally. Several other species of sea-lion, and the closely related fur seals, are found throughout the north and east Pacific and the southern hemisphere. Some were once hunted to the verge of extinction, but fortunately have shown remarkable powers of recovery if properly protected.

WALRUS *Odobenus rosmarus*

A large bull Walrus can reach nearly 3 m long and weigh over 1 tonne. The cows are much smaller but both sexes grow tusks which can be over 1 m long. The Walrus is an Arctic species, occurring around the Arctic coasts of Canada, Alaska and USSR; occasionally odd individuals stray southwards as far as Iceland or even Britain, where they were once regular visitors. They live mainly near the coast and feed on the sea bed on bivalve molluscs and crustaceans, diving to depths of over 70 m. They have large flattened teeth for crushing molluscs, unlike other seals which have pointed teeth for fish eating.

Stiff bristles on the muzzle help locate prey in murky waters. Walrus live in herds, and are migratory, moving south for the winter and north during summer. A single calf is born after a gestation of about 11 months. It can swim soon after birth, but stays with its mother for about 2 years. Walrus live for up to about 30 years in the wild. They have always been of considerable economic importance to Arctic peoples, but during the 17th and 18th century commercial hunting for both ivory and oil exterminated many populations and reduced others. Walruses have been kept in many zoos, but only comparatively recently with success. One kept in New York Zoo ate 140 lbs of fish a day.

COMMON SEAL *Phoca vitulina*

male

Common Seal

female

pup

The Common or Harbour Seal is comparatively small, growing to a maximum of about 2 m and a weight of 150 kg. It is found in coastal waters in the north Atlantic and north Pacific and also in a number of freshwater lakes, including the Seal and Harrison Lakes in Quebec. The pups are born in spring or summer, often on sand banks at low tide, and can swim within a few hours of birth. They are suckled in the water until 3–4 weeks old, when they have to fend for themselves. It is usually these young animals which are found starving and brought to zoos. Common Seals can spend up to 20 minutes under water.

BAIKAL SEAL   *Phoca sibirica*

Common Seal floating

The Baikal Seal is the world's smallest seal, growing to a maximum of about 1.4 m, and is the only one to be entirely confined to fresh water, in Lake Baikal, Siberia. The seals spend the winter beneath the ice of the frozen lake, where the temperature of the water can be 40°C warmer than that of the air above. They keep breathing holes clear of ice, and in late winter the females emerge from the water to make dens in snowdrifts on the ice, where they give birth to 1 or 2 pups. The Baikal Seal is closely related to the Ringed Seal of the Arctic and to the Caspian Seal, and also to the Larga and Common Seals, some populations of which occur in land-locked waters. It has suffered in recent years from the increasing pollution of Lake Baikal by timber processing plants, and in the past has been hunted extensively for its pelt. Baikal Seals are now rarely seen in zoos outside the Soviet Union, although they were once popular exhibits.

Baikal Seal

GREY SEAL *Haliochoerus grypus*

Grey Seals are widespread on both sides of the North Atlantic, with their main stronghold in British waters where large numbers breed in colonies on undisturbed beaches on islands, particularly around Scotland, but are now extinct over much of their southern range in Brittany, the Netherlands and the Baltic. Bulls grow to a maximum of 3 m (usually about 2.3 m from head to tail) and weigh up to 280 kg; the cows are smaller. They are earless seals, of which there are 19 species, mostly found in the cooler waters of the world. They appear earless, for their ears are small and lack obvious ear flaps. Unlike the eared seals, or sea-lions, they cannot turn their flippers and are consequently particularly awkward on land. Grey Seals feed on a wide variety of fish and other marine animals. A single pup is born after a gestation of nearly a year, and is white at birth. Pups are sometimes abandoned on the coast; the mother stops nursing them when they are about 2–3 weeks old. Left to fend for itself, the pup lives off its considerable fat reserves and leaves the breeding beaches after it has moulted, by which time it may be 4–5 weeks old. These apparently abandoned pups – and many do undoubtedly starve – are often brought to zoos. Grey Seals live for 20–30 years in the wild and have lived for 41 years in a zoo; they will breed in captivity.

Monk Seals, superficially similar to Grey Seals, and among the rarest in the world, occur in warmer waters. The Caribbean Monk Seal is extinct and the Mediterranean and Hawaiian species are endangered.

ELEPHANT SEALS

Elephant Seals may weigh nearly as much as an elephant. A mature bull can reach over 3 tonnes and be about 5 m long. There are 2 species. The Southern Elephant Seal *Mirounga leonina*, found on sub-Antarctic islands and the coast of Patagonia, is the larger. The Northern *M. angustirostris* is confined to North America centred around the Santa Barbara Islands and islands off California and Mexico. Both feed in deep water (up to 600 m of more) and can dive for over 10 minutes. They eat a variety of fish which they swallow whole: to digest their prey they have a long gut, sometimes over 200 m long. Although

Northern Elephant Seal

male

female

230

Elephant Seals are mainly solitary at sea, during the breeding season they are very gregarious and crowd together, the males forming harems. Males start to develop their elephant-like proboscis when they are 2 years old, but it is not fully developed for about another 6 years. It is inflated only during the breeding season, when it may function as a resonator to amplify the male's roar when defending his territory. During the 19th century both species were exploited for oil, and almost extinct by 1900. Under protection, they have largely recovered and are once again locally abundant. The Southern Elephant Seal is more common in zoos. It has occasionally bred in captivity, where one has lived for 15 years.

Southern Elephant Seal · males fighting

BOTTLE-NOSED DOLPHIN
Tursiops truncatus

The Bottle-nosed Dolphin is one of the commonest and most widespread dolphins in the Atlantic, India and South Pacific oceans. In the North Pacific it is replaced by a very closely related species, Gill's Bottle-nosed Dolphin *T. gilli*. Bottle-nosed Dolphins grow to about 4 m and a weight of up to 200 kg, but occasionally as much as 650 kg. In the wild they live in groups which may number 3–15, but may join together to form huge schools; up to 1000 have been recorded. A single calf is born after a gestation of 12 months, and suckled (under water) for 12–18 months; females reach maturity at 5–12 years, males 9–13 years old. Bottle-nosed Dolphins are the most popular species of dolphin to be exhibited in zoos and aquaria. They were first kept successfully over a century ago, and are now regularly bred in captivity, though not on a sustained basis – the majority are still wild caught. In captivity they eat between 6 and 7 kg a day.

A number of other dolphins are exhibited in zoos and aquaria. These include the Pacific White-sided Dolphin *Lagenorhynchus obliquidens*, which has been trained to leap exceptionally high, and even in the wild sometimes turns complete somersaults, the Common Dolphin *Delphinus delphis*, and the Spinner Dolphins *Stenella* spp. are also commonly exhibited, particularly in America and Japan. In addition a number of the lesser known species, such as river dolphins, Beluga and Narwhal are exhibited from time to time.

KILLER WHALE *Orcinus orca*

The Killer Whale or Orca, is the largest of the dolphins, and often described as a 'sea wolf', because of its predatory habits. Adult males grow to over 9 m, though females are smaller and less heavily built. In the sea their most distinctive characteristic is the large (up to 1.8 m), erect, triangular dorsal fin; for reasons not entirely understood, in captivity the dorsal fin is not so erect. They live in all oceans and adjoining seas, in groups which range in size from small family groups of 5–20 up to herds of 150 or more. They are very fast swimmers, reaching speeds of over 25 knots, and feed on a wide variety of marine animals including fish, squid, marine turtles, penguins, sea-birds, seals, sea-lions, and whales and dolphins. Packs of Killer Whales hunt larger dolphins and whales up to the size of Minke and Grey Whale calves. However, there does not appear to be any authentic account of a Killer Whale attacking man, without provocation, though divers wearing wetsuits must look remarkably like seals or dolphins. A single calf is born after a gestation of 13–16 months. Killer Whales are popular exhibits in zoos and aquaria, but they are the largest cetacean normally kept in captivity and only a few have the necessary facilities. In captivity they eat about 45 kg a day. They are easily trained to perform a wide variety of 'tricks' and can often perform within 2 months of capture. Killer Whales are hunted in many parts of the world, and although not endangered have declined in many areas. In the wild they probably live for a maximum of over 50 years.

MANATEES

American Manatee

There are 3 closely related species of Manatee: the American Manatee *Trichechus manatus* which is found in coastal waters from Florida south through the Caribbean to Guyana, generally in water with a temperature of about 21°C. The Amazon Manatee *T. inunguis* occurs in the Amazon Basin and adjacent coastal waters; and the African Manatee *T. senegalensis* from coastal waters and rivers from Senegal to Angola. The related Dugong *Dugong dugong* occurs in the Indian Ocean and Australian waters. They all belong to the family Sirenia or Sea Cows and are entirely aquatic, browsing on aquatic plants. Because of their enormous appetites, manatees have been introduced into canals to clear them of choking water weeds such as the water hyacinth. In captivity the American Manatee eats between 30 and 50 kg of vegetation a day. It can grow to a length of 4.5 m and a weight of 1000 kg, but is usually smaller. Manatees swim by moving the large spatulate tail up and down. A single calf is born under water after a gestation of about 1 year; is weaned at about 1 year, and is sexually mature at about 9 years. All manatees are threatened, and many populations are endangered, or even locally extinct. In the past they were hunted in very large numbers for their meat and oil, and as recently as 1950 some 38,000 Amazon Manatees were killed in a single year. One of the main threats to the American Manatee in Florida and the Caribbean comes from boat propellors. Manatees are occasionally kept in zoos and aquaria but rarely breed. They have lived for over 30 years in captivity.

AFRICAN ELEPHANT *Loxodonta africana*

Within historic times the African Elephant occurred almost throughout the length and breadth of Africa, except in the extreme desert regions of the Sahara and Namibia. It is the largest living land animal, standing up to 4 m at the shoulder, with a length of up to 7.5 m (including trunk), plus a tail of up to 1.3 m; it weighs up to 7.5 tonnes, but usually less; males are larger than females. The trunk is a highly modified nose, and has a finger-like end which can be used to pick up food, and other objects. The ears of the

African Elephant are up to 1.5 m long – much larger than those of the Asiatic Elephant. African Elephants live in groups led by females (cows), but may congregate into larger herds, especially at the approach of the rainy season. Mature males form separate herds, and old males may become solitary. A single young (occasionally twins) is born after a gestation of 22 months, weighing up to 135 kg. The young is suckled for 2 years or more. They continue to grow for up to 25 or more years and their life expectancy is 50–70 years. They have been trained in similar ways to Asiatic Elephants; the war elephants of the Carthaginians, with which Hannibal crossed the Alps, were African Elephants and in 1910 a training centre was established in the Belgian Congo, which still exists in present-day Zaire. African Elephants, considered less trustworthy than Asiatic Elephants in captivity, are generally less popular as zoo animals. However, a few of the larger Safari Parks and Zoos are now successfully keeping African Elephants, and have even bred small numbers.

ASIATIC OR INDIAN ELEPHANT
Elephas maxima

Within historic times the Asiatic Elephant occurred from Syria across Asia south of the Himalayas to China and Indochina and south to Sri Lanka, the Malay Peninsula and Sumatra. Its present range is considerably reduced: extinct west of India, it is still found in India, Sri Lanka, Thailand, Burma, Malaysia, China, Vietnam, Borneo, Sumatra and a few adjacent areas. It is smaller than the African Elephant, standing up to 3 m at the shoulder, and growing to a total length (including trunk) of 6.4 m, plus a tail of 1.5 m, and weighing up to 5000 kg. The Asiatic Elephant has smaller ears than the African, and like the African Elephant it often carries tusks, which are modified upper incisors. Whereas both sexes of African Elephant usually have tusks, only the male normally has tusks in the Asiatic. It has been domesticated both for work in forestry, hunting and as a war animal (though this latter use is now purely ceremonial). However, they have not been truly domesticated, but rather wild animals captured, tamed and trained. A single calf is born after a gestation of up to 668 days, weighing up to 150 kg; at birth the calf is covered in brownish hair, and even when adult they are often sparsely haired. They reach sexual maturity at 9–12 years and a captive Asiatic Elephant has lived for 69 years. Like the African Elephant the Asiatic has been hunted extensively for its ivory and it has been estimated that there may be fewer than 28,000 Asiatic Elephants left in their entire range.

AFRICAN WILD ASS   *Equus africanus*

The African Wild Ass is one of the rarest animals in the world. It was once found throughout most of the open areas of northern Africa, but is now confined to a few restricted areas in Somalia and Ethiopia. The African Wild Ass is the ancestor of the domesticated donkey *Equus a. asinus*, which now lives in the wild in some parts of the Wild Ass's former range and has also gone wild in many other parts of the world including the southern USA, where they are known as *burros*. Donkeys are also used in creating hybrids with horses which are known as mules. Mules are usually, though not necessarily, sterile. The African Wild Ass is found in semi-desert areas and is mostly active in the cooler parts of the day and at night, spending the day wherever shade can be found. The males are usually solitary, or live in bachelor herds;

Onager

the females live in small herds with their young. The single young (foal) is born after a gestation of up to 1 year, and is active within a few hours. During the first few days of their life they do not have any flight reflex, and are consequently easy prey to leopards, hyenas and other predators, particularly as the mother often leaves the foal alone while she forages. They reach maturity at 1 year, and females have their first foal when 3 or more years old, males first hold territories at 5–7 years. Domestic donkeys have lived over 40 years, but it is unlikely that in the wild, asses live more than 20. Although donkeys are no longer the common domestic animal that they were, they are still popular in children's zoos. African Wild Asses are comparatively rare in zoos, but there are small populations, most of which have been bred in captivity, and which are slowly growing.

domesticated donkey

243

ZEBRAS

Common Zebra

There are 3 living species of zebra: the Common Zebra *Equus burchelli*, Grevy's Zebra *E. grevyi* and the Mountain Zebra *E. zebra*. A fourth, the Quagga *E. quagga*, became extinct in 1883. The Common Zebra is found in open country from southern Ethiopia to South Africa. Although considerably reduced and fragmented in its range it is still by far the most abundant of the zebras; Grevy's Zebra is confined to arid open areas near the borders of Ethiopia, Somalia and Kenya where it is becoming increasingly rare, and the Mountain Zebra occurs in two quite separate populations: the Cape Mountain Zebra *E. zebra zebra* which nearly became extinct earlier this century but is now slowly recovering in the Mountain Zebra National Park, and Hartmann's Mountain Zebra *E. zebra hartmannae*, which has declined from about 100,000 just after World War II to under 7000 by 1980. In the wild the Common Zebra is one of the characteristic animals of the African Plains. Both sexes grow to a length of up to 2.4 m and stand up to 1.4 m at the shoulder; the tail is about 50 cm long and they weigh up to 335 kg. They live in groups of 1 stallion with up to 6 mares. The single foal is born after a gestation of about 1 year, and is active soon after birth. In captivity Common Zebra have lived up to 40 years.

Grevy's Zebra

WILD HORSE *Equus ferus*

The Wild Horse or Tarpan is probably extinct in the wild, although a few of the eastern race known as the Przewalski's Horse *E. ferus przewalskii* may survive in Mongolia and Sinkiang, but these may have interbred with domestic horses. Many almost pure-bred animals survive in captivity. The Tarpan occurred in Europe and western Asia and has become extinct within historical times. In western Europe it was extinct by the Middle Ages, but a remnant survived in southern Russia until the nineteenth century when these too were exterminated. Przewalski's horse is a rather heavily built, sandy coloured horse with a stiff mane. The breeding biology of wild horses is similar to domestic horses: they give birth to a single foal (occasionally twins) after a gestation of 11 months, and the foal follows the

mother within a few hours of birth. At the turn of the century several Przewalski's horses were captured and imported into Europe, and they formed the basis of all the animals in zoos, where there are thriving herds and the population is rapidly increasing. Many zoos also exhibit various domestic horses, usually the small varieties such as Shetland ponies or Argentine dwarf horses. Some of the rarest domestic horses are the large breeds of 'heavy' horses, formerly used for ploughing and pulling carts. In several parts of the world domestic horses have been released or escaped to become feral. Those of the uplands of Britain, such as the Exmoor, are fairly primitive horses, while others, such as those of the New Forest, have been 'improved' by cross-breeding with thoroughbreds. In America large herds of 'mustangs', perhaps descended from the ponies brought by the Conquistadores, roam the more remote parts of the southern states. In the nineteenth century the herds were very large, but have declined with loss of habitat as well as by hunting. Attempts have been made to recreate the extinct Tarpan by inbreeding horses with primitive characteristics and these experiments have been successful in as much as animals closely resemble the Tarpan now exist. Some have been released into semi-natural conditions and others are kept in zoos.

TAPIRS

Malayan Tapir

Brazilian Tapir

There are 4 species of tapir, 3 of which are found in tropical South America and 1 in south-east Asia. They are hoofed mammals, related to horses and rhinoceros, having an uneven number of toes. Tapirs are mainly browsers, feeding on leaves and shoots, and also aquatic vegetation and occasionally grazing on crops. All 4 species are exhibited in zoos and have been bred in captivity. The most commonly exhibited tapirs are the Malayan and the Brazilian. The most widespread of the South American species is the Brazilian Tapir *Tapirus terrestris* which is found from Colombia and Venezuela south to southern Brazil and Argentina; Baird's Tapir *T. bairdi* is found from Mexico south to Ecuador and the Mountain Tapir *T. roulini* (= *pinchaque*) in the Andes from Colombia to northern Peru, at altitudes above 2000 m (6500 ft). The number of both Baird's and the Mountain Tapir are declining.

The Malayan Tapir *T. indicus* is found from Burma, south through Thailand and the Malay Peninsula to Sumatra; it is now very rare over most of its range. The Malayan Tapir grows to a length of up to about 2.25 m (the tail is insignificant) and weighs up to 375 kg. A single calf is born after a gestation of about 390 days and like the Brazilian tapir it is heavily striped. The females probably give birth in alternate years, and in captivity a male has lived to over 30 years of age. In the wild tapirs are often hunted for food and they have also become rare as their forest habitats have been cleared for agriculture.

ASIAN RHINOCEROS

Indian Rhino

Sumatran Rhino

Javan Rhino

The 3 species of Asian Rhinoceros are much rarer than the African species and considered endangered. Only the Indian Rhino *Rhinoceros unicornis* is normally seen in zoos. Once found over much of northern India, Nepal, Assam and northern Pakistan, it is now confined to a few reserves, of which the most important are Kaziranga in Assam and Chitawan in Nepal. Indian Rhinos grow to a length of 4.2 m, shoulder height of 2 m and weight of up to 400 g. Easily distinguished from African rhinos by their skin, which hangs in loose armour-like folds, they live in tall grass and swampy jungles, rarely going far from water, in which they wallow. The single young is born after a gestation of about 16 months. Its life span is estimated at 50 years or more.

The Javan Rhino *R. sondaicus*, closely related to, though much smaller than, the Indian Rhino, was once fairly widespread from eastern India to southern China, south to Java. Now one of the most endangered of all animals, the only certain survivors are in the Udjung Kulon Reserve, Java.

The Sumatran or Hairy Rhino *Dicerorhinus sumatrensis*, once found from Assam and Bengal to Vietnam and south to Borneo, now occurs only in small, scattered populations over a much reduced range. Its front horn is inconspicuous and the second horn also rather short. No Sumatran or Javan Rhinos are currently in zoos but the only hope for their survival may depend on some being captured to start a captive breeding programme.

BLACK RHINOCEROS *Diceros bicornis*

The Black Rhino was at one time widespread throughout Africa south of the Sahara but, outside East Africa, is now restricted to a few isolated and scattered populations. In the last few years many East

African populations have also been exterminated and most of those surviving are under considerable poaching pressure. The Black Rhino grows to a maximum length of up to 3.5 m, a shoulder height of 2.25 m and a weight of 1600 kg; the front of 2 horns grows to a length of up to 80 cm, rarely up to 120 cm. Almost exclusively a browser, the Black Rhino's pointed and prehensile lip, which it uses to grasp leaves of bushes and shrubs, distinguish it from the White, which is a grazer. Black Rhinos live in quite thickly wooded country, forest edges and more open shrub and thorn country, usually close to a permanent water supply. Like other rhinos they are rather short-sighted and rely on their senses of hearing and smell, often charging unknown sounds and smells;

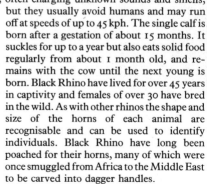

but they usually avoid humans and may run off at speeds of up to 45 kph. The single calf is born after a gestation of about 15 months. It suckles for up to a year but also eats solid food regularly from about 1 month old, and remains with the cow until the next young is born. Black Rhino have lived for over 45 years in captivity and females of over 30 have bred in the wild. As with other rhinos the shape and size of the horns of each animal are recognisable and can be used to identify individuals. Black Rhino have long been poached for their horns, many of which were once smuggled from Africa to the Middle East to be carved into dagger handles.

Jambia with a rhino horn handle

WHITE OR SQUARE-LIPPED RHINOCEROS *Ceratotherium simum*

The White Rhinoceros formerly occurred in 2 separate parts of Africa: the Northern White Rhino *C.s. cottoni* below the Sahara from Chad to the Sudan and south to north-east Zaire and north-west Uganda; the Southern White Rhino *C.s. simum* in south-east Angola, south-west Zambia, Mozambique, Zimbabwe, Botswana and South Africa. It is now extinct over much of its range and very few of the Northern White survive. Under strict protection the Southern White has flourished in South Africa and has been introduced into a number of national parks in Kenya and Zimbabwe, as well as being exported to zoos. The White Rhino is surpassed in size only by the elephant. A fully grown bull can weigh up to 3600 kg, stand over 2 m at the shoulder and be up to 3.8 m long. White Rhinos have 2 horns, of which the front one grows to about 1 m, occasionally over 1.5 m; females' horns are longer and thinner than those of males. The name White is derived from the Africaans *weit* meaning wide, referring to its square lip, the Black Rhino having a narrow pointed lip. White Rhinos are found in bush and savannah, usually with trees and access to water, where they feed mainly on short grass. The single calf is born after a gestation of about 16–18 months, suckled for about a year and remains with its mother for 2–3 years, leaving only when the next calf is born. A wild female has been recorded as breeding at 36 years of age. White Rhinos have no enemies other than man. Their present rarity is due mainly to poaching for their horn, highly prized in the far east as a medicine, particularly for treating fevers, and in various parts of Asia for carving. There are many Southern Whites in captivity, often breeding freely, but only a handful of the Northern subspecies.

Powdered rhino horn is highly valued in oriental medicine

HYRAXES

Cape Dassie

Tree Hyrax

The 5 living species of hyraxes or dassies are quite unlike any other mammals and placed in their own Order, Hyracoidea. They are often described as being closely related to elephants – in reality all that is likely is that both elephants and hyraxes may share a common ancestor. They are mostly found in Africa, but have also spread into the Mediterranean area, and are the Conies mentioned in the Bible.

The hyrax most frequently seen in zoos is the Cape

Dassie or Large-toothed Rock Hyrax *Procavia capensis*. It is widespread in most open habitats in Africa south of the Sahara and also northwards to Egypt, the Levant and Arabia. It grows to a length of up to 57 cm and a weight of 5 kg. Dassies inhabit rocky hillsides, ravines and kloofs, where they are colonial. They do not move far from cover and emerge in the morning and evening to sunbathe. They have look-out points, from which the alarm call is whistled, and also well-used walkways and easily recognised latrine areas. Up to 6 young are born fully furred with their eyes open, after a gestation of about 240 days, and are active within a day of birth. They suckle for up to 5 months, but leave the breeding hole after 3 months, and are not normally sexually mature until their second year. They are preyed on by a wide range of animals, including Leopards and other cats, eagles and large snakes. In areas where Leopards and other predators have been exterminated Dassies have increased to pest proportions, damaging crops. They make active and interesting exhibits in zoos, where they often breed fairly freely and have lived for up to 12 years. Other species of hyrax, such as the 3 species of tree hyraxes *Dendrohyrax* and the Small-toothed Hyrax, are more rarely seen in zoos.

AARDVARK *Orycteropus afer*

The Aardvark or Ant Bear has a wide range in Africa, south of the Sahara, occurring almost everywhere with a suitable habitat, although in recent years it has declined in many areas. It grows to a length of up to 1.5 m, plus a tapering tail of up to 60 cm, and it weighs up to 80 kg. Aardvarks have evolved several modifications to enable them to dig for termites: they have powerful claws, the nostrils at the end of the long snout are protected by stiff hairs and the long tubular ears can be folded back.

Aardvarks are nocturnal, and spend the day in a tunnel which they excavate, blocking the entrance except for an air vent. Although they feed mainly on termites, they also take other insects and their larvae and the fungi which grows in termite colonies; they also seek out wild cucumbers, the seeds of which need to be partly digested before they can germinate. A single young (occasionally twins) is born in a nest in a burrow after a gestation of 7 months, and is pink and hairless at birth. After about 2 weeks the young accompanies the mother foraging, and after about 6 months the young starts digging for itself. In captivity an Aardvark has lived for 23 years.

The abandoned burrows of Aardvarks provide homes and shelter for a wide range of other wildlife including bats, ground squirrels, porcupines, monitor lizards, pythons, jackals, hyenas and owls. Although their thick skins protect them from termite and other insect bites, Aardvarks have many enemies, particularly when young; they are preyed on by Leopard, Lion, hyenas, hunting dogs and even pythons. When attacked they usually try to run away or dig themselves into the ground, but an Aardvark will also defend itself with its forefeet. Aardvarks are comparatively unusual in zoos, but have been bred on several occasions, and for more than one generation.

WILD BOAR *Sus scrofa*

The Wild Boar, the ancestor of the domestic pig, was once found over most of Europe, North Africa and eastwards across to Japan and south-east Asia. In its domestic forms it has also been extensively introduced or escaped; feral and wild pigs now occur in New Guinea, New Zealand, many oceanic islands and some parts of Africa, North and South America. Wild boar grow up to 1.8 m long, stand 1 m at the shoulder and weigh up to 230 kg; males (boars) are larger than females (sows), and have protruding tusks, which can grow to 30 cm. Wild Boar occur in a wide variety of usually wooded habitats, and eat mainly vegetable foods. They often feed on man's crops and can cause extensive damage. They are hunted for sport and in many parts of their range (notably Britain) have been exterminated. Wild boar normally live alone or in small groups ('sounders'), but sometimes in groups of 100 or more. They are mainly active at night and twilight, hiding in dense cover by day. After a gestation of up to 140 days a litter of up to 12 piglets is born in spring or early summer in a rough nest, built by the mother, which they leave after a few days. They are weaned at 3–4 months and become sexually mature at 8–10 months. In Thailand they may have been domesticated nearly 12,000 years ago, but the domestic pigs of Europe were often very boar-like until the 18th century, when they were cross-bred with oriental pigs. Many zoos exhibit Vietnamese pot-bellied pigs or similar breeds. The introduction of domestic pigs on to oceanic islands has been responsible for the decline and even extinction of many species; the most famous is the Dodo, of Mauritius. Wild Boar are often exhibited in zoos and many live up to 20 years in captivity.

WARTHOG *Phacochoerus aethiopicus*

The Warthog is widespread in suitable habitat over most of Africa, south of the Sahara. Its preferred habitat includes woodlands, savannahs, scrub and swamps and it also occurs in more open plains and mountainous habitats up to 2500 m (8125 ft). The Warthog grows to 1.5 m, plus a tail of 45 cm, and weighs up to 150 kg; the male is larger than the female and has longer tusks, growing up to 60 cm. Unlike most other pigs they are mainly active during the daytime. They feed mainly on vegetable matter including roots and rhizomes, grasses, fruits and berries and occasionally carrion. They live in small groups which may band together to form much larger groups of up to 40. Adult males are usually solitary, only joining females for mating, when they fight other males. These fights are ritualized: they strike each other with their head, the warts softening the

blows. After a gestation of up to 175 days a litter of 2–4 (occasionally up to 8) is born, in a burrow. At 7 weeks old the young accompany the mother. In captivity a Warthog has lived over 18 years. Although Warthogs are one of the commonest pigs in Africa, they are not all that often seen in zoos, and only breed infrequently in captivity.

Three other species of wild pigs are found in Africa: the Wild Boar (p. 260), the Bush Pig *Potamochoerus porcus* and the Giant Forest Hog *Hylochoerus meinertzhageni*. The Bush Pig (or Red River Hog) is sometimes exhibited in zoos. It is found in more forested areas than the Warthog, over much of Africa, south of the Sahara. The Bush Pig has recently increased with the spread of agriculture (it often feeds on crops) and the extermination of predators such as Leopard. The Giant Forest Hog, was one of the last large mammals to be discovered in Africa. It grows to a length of up to 1.8 m, stands up to 1 m high at the shoulder and weighs up to 250 kg. It is found in forests from Liberia to Kenya and southern Ethiopia, but its range is still not properly known, nor much known of its habits. It is unlikely to be seen in zoos.

PECCARIES

Collared Peccary

The peccaries are the New World equivalents of the pigs. There are 3 species: the Collared Peccary *Tayassu tajacu*, which is the most widespread, occurring from the southern states of the USA, south through Central and South America to northern Argentina; the White-lipped Peccary *Tayassu pecari* which occurs in forests from southern Mexico south to northern Argentina and the Chaco Peccary *Catagonus wagneri*, which was only discovered as a living animal in the 1970s, and is confined to the

Gran Chaco area on the borders of Bolivia, Paraguay and Argentina. The Collared Peccary lives in a wide variety of habitats including semi-desert, rain forest and swamps. They grow to a length of just under 1 m (the tail of about 3 cm is not easily visible), stand up to 60 cm at the shoulder and weigh up to 27 kg, usually less. They are social animals, living in mixed age and sex groups of 2–15, occasionally up to 50. They search for food among forest litter and soil with their snout and can smell food even when it is several cms below the surface. They feed on mostly plant matter including cacti fruit, forbs, grasses, seeds and nuts, and only occasionally animals or carrion are eaten. The female produces a litter of 1–4 (usually 2) after a gestation of 115 days, in a nest under a log or in a burrow. Within a few days they follow their mother when she rejoins the herd. The young mature rapidly and in captivity they are capable of breeding when they are only 33 weeks old, but in the wild they are nearly a year old when they first breed. Collared Peccaries are exhibited in many zoos, and they are frequently bred in captivity and have been bred for many generations.

HIPPOPOTAMI

Hippopotamus

The Hippopotamus *Hippopotamus amphibius* was once widely distributed in Africa south of the Sahara in almost all areas with suitable aquatic habitats. Within historic times it occurred in the Nile (and was often depicted by Ancient Egyptians) and during the Pleistocene Period was found as far north as southern England. Its range now considerably reduced and fragmented, it is still locally abundant. Hippos grow to a length of up to 4.6 m, a shoulder height of 1.5 m and a weight of 4500 kg. Canine teeth, enlarged into 'tusks', may weigh 3 kg and are often used as a substitute for elephant or walrus ivory. Hippos spend most of the day sleeping submerged in water with only ears, eyes and nostrils exposed. At night they leave the water to graze and may travel 3 km or more to grazing sites. Normally harmless, Hippos can be dangerous if their retreat to water is cut off. They breed at all times of the year; the single calf (rarely twins) is born after a gestation of up to 8 months. The new-born calves can swim before they can walk and suckle under water. In the wild the average life span when not hunted by man) is 41 years. They breed regularly in captivity.

The Pygmy Hippopotamus *Choeropsis liberiensis* is restricted to isolated areas in West Africa, from Sierra Leone to Nigeria. Very much smaller than the Hippopotamus, it grows to a maximum length of 1.7 m, a height of 1 m, and a weight of 270 kg. It is less aquatic and found mainly near streams and rivers in wet forests and swamps. The Pygmy Hippos is comparatively rare in the wild and classified as vulnerable but there is a substantial zoo population, mostly bred in captivity, where one has lived for over 38 years.

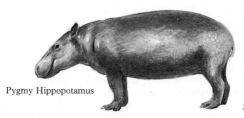

Pygmy Hippopotamus

GUANACO AND VICUNA

Guanacos

The Guanaco *Lama guanicoe* is thought to be the wild ancestor of both the Llama *L. glama*, and the Alpaca *L. pacos* (p. 264). They grow to a length of up to 2.25 m, a shoulder height of 1.3 m and a weight of 140 kg. Guanaco inhabit dry, open countryside from southern Peru to eastern Argentina and south to Tierra del Fuego. They live in small herds led by a male. The female gives birth to a single young every other year after a gestation of 10–11 months. A Guanaco has lived for over 28 years in captivity.

The Vicuna *Vicugna vicugna*, smaller and more lightly built than the Guanaco and its domesticated relatives, grows to a length of 1.9 m, standing 1.1 m at the shoulder and weighing under 65 kg. It is found in the Andes of southern Peru, Argentina, Bolivia and Chile, in rather arid grasslands at latitudes of 3500–5750 m, living in small groups led by a male, males also form bachelor herds or live singly. A single young, born after a gestation of 11 months, can walk $\frac{1}{4}$ hour after birth and is weaned at about 10 months. Vicunas have lived over 24 years in captivity. During the Inca rule the Vicuna was very widespread and it was estimated that $1-1\frac{1}{2}$ million Vicuna were periodically rounded up and sheared for their exceptionally fine wool. After the Spanish Conquest, they were slaughtered for meat and wool. By the 1950s there were still about 400,000 left, but the high value of the wool led to further hunting until there was less than 10,000 in the 1960s. Subsequent protection has enabled them to recover and there are now probably over 80,000.

Vicuna

ALPACA AND LLAMA *Lama guanicoe*

The Alpaca and Llama are generally thought to have
descended from the Guanaco, but have been domesticated for so long (about 4500 years) that they are
often treated as separate species. The Alpaca is
primarily bred for its wool and even today the Alpaca,
which is ideally adapted to the harsh environment of
the Andes, is a major producer of wool. The animals
are only shorn every other year, each animal producing just under 3 kg of wool. Their biology is similar to
that of the wild Guanacos.

The Llama is primarily a beast of burden, and as
such was extremely important in the days of the Inca
empire: it has never entirely lost its importance and
even today in mountainous terrain it is used to carry

Alpaca

loads of up to 45 kg, at altitudes over 2000 m. Traditionally only males over about 3 years old are used as pack animals, the females being kept for wool and for breeding. In addition to their use as pack animals, Llamas supplied many of the needs of the Indians of the Andes: rugs from the fur, leather and sandals from the hide, meat, tallow from the fat, and even fuel from the dung. The Llama, and its relatives, deposit their dung at certain well-marked sites, which can accumulate heaps up to 30 cm deep and 2.5 m across. Llamas will interbreed with Guanaco and Alpaca, and they are commonly seen in zoos. However, although in their native South America many different varieties have been bred, most of those in zoos are of no particular breed, and it is likely that many of the breeds in South America are becoming rare as motorised transport becomes more widely available.

Llamas

CAMELS

There are two species of Camel: the Dromedary or
Arabian Camel *Camelus dromedarius* and the
Bactrian Camel *C. ferus* (= *bactrianus*). They live in
arid areas where they can survive for long periods
without drinking, obtaining moisture from vegetation, including salty plants. They can drink as much
as 57 litres to replenish their body fluids. The female
usually gives birth to a single calf (rarely twins) every
other year after a gestation of up to 440 days. The
young are fully independent at 4 years old and fully
grown at 5. They can live up to 50 years. Camels grow
to about 3.5 m long, a shoulder height of 2.1 m and a
weight of 690 kg. They have a characteristic rolling

Dromedary

gait, caused by moving the fore and hind legs together on each side; they can run at 65 kph.

The single-humped Dromedary was domesticated perhaps as early as 4000 BC. The wild form, found in Arabia and possibly North Africa, either became extinct nearly 2000 years ago or was gradually absorbed into the domestic herds. Dromedaries have been introduced into many parts of the world, including southern USA, south and east Africa, Spain and Australia (where a large feral population still exists). The Bactrian or Two-humped Camel also has a long history as a domestic animal, back to the 3rd or 4th century BC. Until the 1920s its range was extensive and it was locally abundant from Asia Minor, through central Asia to China, but is now restricted to southwestern Mongolia and western China where about 300–500 survive.

Bactrian Camel

CHEVROTAINS

Indian Spotted Chevrotain

There are 3 species of chevrotain, or Mouse Deer: the Lesser Malay Chevrotain *Tragulus javanicus* from Indo-China south to Java and Borneo; the Indian Spotted Chevrotain *T. neminna* from India and Sri Lanka and the Greater Malay Chevrotain *T. napu*, from southern Thailand and Indo-China south to Sumatra and Borneo. A fourth closely related species, the Water Chevrotain *Hyemoschus aquaticus* is found in Africa. The species most frequently seen in captivity is the Lesser Malay Chevrotain which grows to a length of 48 cm, and weighs up to 2 kg.

Chevrotains are the smallest of the hoofed animals, smaller even than Dik-diks and Royal Antelope. They are mainly nocturnal, usually living alone or in pairs, in dense forest where they are shy and secretive, making tiny tunnel-like trails in the forest. They also hide in rock clefts and hollow trees. They are browsers and grazers feeding on low bushes, grasses and fallen fruits. The single young (occasionally 2) is active soon after birth – within 30 minutes it can stand on its own – and mature at about 5 months. Unlike many other hoofed animals the Chevrotains have 4 well developed toes on each foot. They lack horns or antlers but have well developed upper canines (especially the males). Chevrotains are often very numerous, but are rarely seen. They have many enemies and are preyed on by snakes and most larger carnivorous mammals and are often hunted by man for food. All three Asian Chevrotains are occasionally seen in zoos, and are bred in small numbers. A Greater Malay Chevrotain has lived for over 14 years in captivity. They tame easily and are often kept as pets in Malaya, where they play the same role in local folklore as the fox in Europe.

Lesser Malay Chevrotain

CHINESE WATER DEER *Hydropotes inermis*

The Chinese Water Deer is found in eastern
central China and Korea, and has also been
introduced into Britain and France. It is a
small deer, lacking antlers, but with the upper
canine teeth enlarged into tusks, especially in
the males. Chinese Water Deer grow to about
1 m long, stand about 55 cm at the shoulder
and weigh up to 15 kg. In their native range
they live among reeds and sedges in watery
habitats, and also in tall grasses in more hilly
country. When running they have a bounding
gait, rather like that of a hare. They feed on
grasses water plants and roots. In Britain, in
addition to habitats similar to their native

range, they also occur in woodlands and even gardens. Chinese Water Deer are normally solitary and the males mark their territories with a distinctive musky scent. They are the most prolific of all deer. Young are born in spring after a gestation of 6 months. There are usually 2, sometimes 3 fawns, but 4 or 5 are occasionally born and up to 8 in a single litter are known, though it is doubtful that a female could rear more than 3 or 4. Between World War I and World War II they escaped from those kept in the Duke of Bedford's deer park at Woburn and from Whipsnade Zoo into the English countryside. They have spread slowly, but probably suffer heavy mortality in cold winters, and because of their small size (less than 500 g at birth) are probably heavily predated by foxes and birds of prey. However, they are secretive and almost certainly more widespread than generally realised. It is believed that, even if they become more widespread, they would cause little damage, since they are primarily grazers, rather than browsers. A captive Chinese Water Deer has lived for over 11 years.

Chinese Water Deer are related to the Musk Deer *Moschus* spp. which, although at present rarely seen in zoos, are being farmed in China. They are kept for their musk, which is a wax-like secretion used in the perfume industry. The high prices paid for musk have led to Musk Deer being exterminated in some areas in their native Himalayas and eastern Asia.

MUNTJACS

male in spring

The Muntjacs are small deer from eastern Asia, the Chinese or Reeve's Muntjac *Muntiacus reevesi* occurs in south and east China and on the island of Taiwan. It has also escaped from zoos and been introduced into England and France. The Chinese Muntjac is small, standing only 46 cm at the shoulder and weighing less than 15 kg. The males have short (up to 7.5 cm) antlers, and canine teeth enlarged into small tusks. They are sometimes known as Barking Deer on account of their dog-like calls often heard at dusk and dawn. Both the Chinese Muntjac and the Indian Muntjac *M. muntiak* were kept in captivity in England at the end of the beginning of this century and bred freely. The Duke of Bedford released both species into woodlands and Woburn, and others escaped from Whipsnade Zoo. The Chinese species has now colonised a large part of the more wooded areas of southern England. A single fawn is born after a gestation of up to 220 days and in captivity they have lived over 17 years.

There are also 3 other, rather rare species of Muntjac: the Black Muntjac *M. crinifrons* which was for many years thought to be extinct, but rediscovered in the 1980s in eastern China; Fea's Muntjac *M. feae*, from a small area of Thailand and Tenasserim, which is endangered, and Roosevelt's Muntjac *M. rooseveltorum*, which is only known from one locality in Laos.

Female in winter

CHITAL *Cervus axis*

male

female

Chital (also known as the Axis or Spotted Deer) is one of the most attractive of all deer, looking very much like the deer of fairy stories. They grow to a length of up to 1.7 m, a shoulder height of 1 m and weight of up to 110 kg. The antlers grow to over 1 m in the wild. Chital are usually associated with picturesque scenery, living in woodland glades near rivers and streams. They usually live in herds of up to about 30 animals, which comprise 2 or 3 stags, females and their young. Sometimes herds number 100–200 animals and the herd structure is rather variable. During the rut (the time of which varies depending on locality) the stags fight fiercely. Chital breed during most of the year. A single fawn is born after a gestation of about $5\frac{1}{2}$ months, and usually becomes independent at about 1 year old. They are prolific breeders and a hind may have more than one fawn a year. Chital are found throughout the Indian peninsula and Sri Lanka; they have also been introduced into Yugoslavia and New Zealand, Hawaii, Brazil, Argentina and Florida (USA).

The closely related Hog Deer *C. porcinus* is widespread from north-west India, through southeast Asia to Indonesia and the Philippines; it has also been introduced extensively elsewhere, including Sri Lanka and Australia. Two populations of this deer, from the Calamian Islands *C.p. calamianensis* and Bawean Island *C.p. kuhli* are both threatened but are now being bred in small numbers in captivity. The Axis Deer and Hog Deer are both bred in captivity in large numbers and have been self-sustaining in captivity for many years. A Chital has lived for over 20 years in captivity.

male with antlers in velvet

FALLOW DEER *Cervus dama*

male in autumn, with females

The Fallow Deer is one of the most familiar of all deer and for many centuries has been kept in parks, and has been a popular zoo exhibit in all parts of the world. Originally it occurred in Mediterranean Europe east through Asia Minor to Iran. Since Roman times it has been introduced widely in Europe including Britain and Ireland, and more recently into Africa, North and South America, Australia and New Zealand. In park and zoo herds there is often a wide range of colour variations including albinos and melanistic forms; in winter the spots are lost except in the variety known as 'Menil'. Fallow Deer are about 1.75 m long, stand about 1 m at the shoulder and weigh up to about 100 kg. The spreading, palmate antlers grow to about 76 cm from tip to tip. The single fawn is born after a gestation of approximately 230 days, and is heavily spotted. They reach maturity at about 16 months and live for about 15 years.

The Persian population *C. dama mesopotamica*, is sometimes regarded as a distinct species. It was once thought extinct but about 50 were rediscovered in the 1950s living in swamps on the Iran–Iraq border. In addition to those living in the wild there are small numbers in captivity, which are gradually increasing in number.

female in winter coat

SWAMP DEER *Cervus duvauceli*

The Swamp Deer or Barasingha is found only in India where 2 subspecies occur. *C. duvauceli duvauceli* from the swamps of Terai, Assam and Uttar Pradesh have splayed hooves – suitable for swampy ground – while *C. duvauceli branderi*, which is found in more open grassy areas in Madhya Pradesh, have smaller, well knit hooves. The Swamp Deer stands up to 1.3 m at the shoulder and weighs up to 180 kg. The antlers, which are carried only by the male, grow to a maximum of over 1 m long; the shape of the antlers is extremely variable, with up to 20 points, but more usually 10–14. Swamp deer are often active by day and are less nocturnal than the Sambar (p. 290), which is often found in the same habitat. They usually graze until late morning, lying up during the heat of the day, and emerging again in the evening to feed. They are very gregarious and when the herds are alarmed they run off making a shrill, baying alarm call. In breeding biology the Swamp Deer is similar to the Sambar, Red Deer and other related species. It is one of the rarest deer, and has been heavily overhunted over most of its range and is considered endangered. Fortunately there are substantial numbers in captivity, all of which were probably bred in captivity; however, only a few zoos keep them in herds of more than 10 animals, far fewer than in the herds which they form in the wild.

RED DEER OR WAPITI *Cervus elaphus*

stag

hind

In the Old World the Red Deer is widespread throughout most of Europe and across Asia to Siberia, China and Korea, and south to the Himalayas and North Africa. In North America, where it is known as the Elk or Wapiti, it is widespread in southern Canada and most of the

USA. It has also been introduced into New Zealand and other parts of the world. There is considerable variation in size, largely depending on the quality of the habitat; animals from New Zealand, parts of North America, the Carpathians being among the largest, growing to a shoulder height of 1.5 m, a length of 2.65 m and a weight of up to 340 kg. However, from other parts of their range, such as the Highlands of Scotland, Red Deer are often considerably smaller, weighing as little as 80 kg. They are gregarious, each sex forming separate herds for most of the year. Their preferred habitat is open woodlands, but they are very adaptable. A single calf (occasionally twins) is born after a gestation of up to 9 months, is active soon after birth, and follows the mother when about 3 days old. It is heavily spotted at birth, but moults by about 3 months.

Wapiti stag in winter

SIKA DEER *Cervus nippón*

male in winter

The Sika Deer has an extensive range in eastern Asia from south-east Siberia through eastern China to Japan and Taiwan (Formosa). It is a rather variable species and a number of subspecies have been described. The Sika Deer has also been extensively introduced, and has escaped from parks in many other parts of the world, including New Zealand, England, Ireland, Morocco, USA, USSR and several parts of Europe. There is considerable variation in size; the shoulder height varies between about 86 cm and 188 cm, and the weight between 40 and 140 kg; males are generally longer and heavier than females. Their behaviour is rather variable, some living in herds, others singly or in small groups. The single calf (occasionally twins) is born after a gestation of about 30 weeks, and mature between 16–18 months. Sika Deer are frequently exhibited in zoos, including several of the rarer subspecies. The endangered Formosan Sika *C. nippon taiouanus* is kept in substantial numbers and in Japan several of the island subspecies are kept in zoos. The South China Sika *C.n. kopschi* is very small, standing about 80 cm at the shoulder, this with the Shansi Sika *C.n. grassianus*, the North China Sika *C.n. mandarinensis*, and the Ryukyu Sika *C.n. keramae* are also all endangered, but do not appear to be being bred in captivity.

male with antlers in velvet

adult female

SAMBAR *Cervus unicolor*

The Sambar, or Sambur, is widespread from India eastwards to southern China and south to Sri Lanka, Java, Borneo, Celebes and the Philippines. They have also been introduced into Australia and New

Zealand. The Sambar is a fairly large deer, standing up to 1.5 m at the shoulder; a large stag weighing up to 320 kg. Males carry large antlers – the record is about 1.3 m long. The Sambar of the Philippines are much smaller, standing less than 70 cm at the shoulder and weighing under 60 kg. They are sometimes regarded as a separate species *C. mariannus*. Sambar usually live in small groups, on forested hillsides, often near cultivated areas. They feed on a wide variety of vegetation and are both browsers and grazers. In most areas they are largely nocturnal, feeding at night and hiding in dense vegetation during the daytime. Sambar are good swimmers and often take to the water. The males cast their antlers in March–April and the new ones start to grow during the rainy season, and are clear of velvet by November. The males rub the velvet off against the trees. Each male defends a territory, usually a valley, and each harem contains about 5 or 6 hinds. Outside the rut, the stags are solitary. The single calf (occasionally twins) is born in late May or June at the commencement of the rains, after a gestation of 8–9 months.

Several other similar deer occur in south-east Asia: Schomburgk's Deer *C. schomburgki* from Thailand became extinct about 1938, but the Rusa or Timor Deer *C. timorensis* is widespread in Java, Celebes, Timor and other islands and has been introduced into New Zealand and Australia. Sambar and Rusa are exhibited in many zoos and wildlife parks where they have bred for many generations.

PÈRE DAVID'S DEER *Elaphurus davidianus*

Père David's Deer originally occurred in the low-lands of north-eastern China, but became extinct in the wild nearly 3000 years ago. However, a herd survived enclosed in the Imperial Hunting Park, near Peking until 1900. In 1865 the French missionary and naturalist Father David (after whom the deer is named) was the first European to see them, and later he was able to send some live specimens to Europe where they were dispersed among several zoos. In 1894 a flood breached the walls of the Imperial Hunting Park and the deer escaped, only to be eaten by starving peasants. Six years later most of the remainder were shot by foreign troops during the Boxer Rebellion and by 1911 only two were left in China; by 1921 both were dead. Meanwhile, the Duke of Bedford had gathered together as many as he could at his private zoo at Woburn, England. In 1900

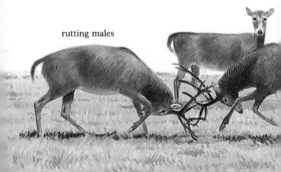

rutting males

and 1901 he gathered 16, and by 1922 his herd had grown to 64. After World War II the Woburn herd had grown large enough to allow others to be established, and by the early 1960s the world total exceeded 400 and four were sent back to China. By the 1980s there were over 1000 dispersed among about 100 collections.

Père David's Deer grows to about 1.5 m, stands about 1.15 m at the shoulder and weighs up to 200 kg. They have large spreading hooves, an adaptation to their original swampy habitat. During the rut the males fight with their antlers and teeth and also rear up on their hind legs and box. One or 2 fawns are born after a gestation of up to 270 days, and maturity is reached at about 27 months. Since its original habitat has completely disappeared it is unlikely that it will ever be possible to release Père David's Deer into truly wild conditions.

male with antlers
shedding velvet

MOOSE OR ELK *Alces alces*

male with antlers
in velvet

In North America known as the Moose, and in
Europe as the Elk, the largest of the deer, it is found in
wooded areas that are covered with snow in winter,
throughout the northern parts of the Old and New
World. The Moose grows to 3.1 m long, standing up
to 2.35 m at the shoulder and weighing up to 825 kg,
but usually much less. The males carry broad
palmate antlers, which grow to a record spread of

over 2 m, and may weigh up to 35 kg. Moose prefer fairly wet habitats, browsing on sallows and willows, and also on aquatic vegetation, eating nearly 20 kg a day. They are generally solitary but males will fight for females during the rut in September–October. After a gestation of up to 264 days 1 or 2 (rarely 3) young are born which stay with the mother for at least a year. They have lived up to 27 years. In the past the range of the Moose was considerably reduced by hunting and it had disappeared from most of Europe and much of the USA. However, under strict protection its numbers have rebuilt and its range is still spreading, with an estimated 2 million in the world by the 1970s. Moose are an important game animal and in Sweden provide a significant part of the national meat production. In Sweden during the last century, and more recently in the USSR, they have been domesticated both for meat and milk, and have also been used as draft animals for pulling carts and sledges.

female

REINDEER OR CARIBOU
Rangifer tarundus

The Reindeer, or Caribou as it is known in North America, was once found throughout the more northerly latitudes of the northern hemisphere on Arctic tundra and in woodlands, but in many of the latter areas it is now extinct. In Europe the wild Reindeer is extinct in Norway and Sweden and endangered in Finland. Within historic times it also occurred in Poland and Germany. Reindeer grow up to 2.2 m long, with a tail of up to 21 cm, a shoulder height of 1.4 m and a maximum weight of 318 kg; males are larger than females. They are the only deer in which both sexes have antlers, which are very variable and grow up to 1.3 m long in males. They have broad, deeply cloven hooves which help when walking on soft snow and marshy ground – when running they can reach speeds of up to 80 kph. Most Reindeer are migratory, moving in herds to the northern latitudes in summer, where the calves are born, after a gestation of about 228 days. The single calf follows the mother an hour after birth, and a day later can run faster than a human. Throughout the Arctic regions Reindeer are hunted by the native peoples and in the Old World have been domesticated for about 3000 years. Even when domesticated, most Reindeer continue to migrate between the summer and winter feeding grounds. Although wild Reindeer are threatened in many parts of their range, there are probably more than 3 million domesticated animals. Reindeer have been introduced into the Cairngorms (Scotland), South Georgia, the Kerguelen Islands, Iceland and Greenland. Their maximum life span in the wild is about 13 years, but a Reindeer has lived for over 20 years in captivity.

domesticated female Reindeer and Laplander

WHITE-TAILED DEER
Odocoileus virginianus

The White-tailed Deer is widespread over much of the Americas from southern Canada southwards to Peru and northern Brazil, and has been introduced into New Zealand, Cuba and other parts of North America. In the western parts of its range it overlaps with or is replaced by the Mule or Black-tailed Deer, *O. hemionus*. The White-tailed Deer grows to a length of about 2.4 m, stands up to 1 m and weighs up to 192 kg. However, there is considerable variation and these maxima apply to the subspecies *O.*

virginianus borealis; the Florida Keys White-tailed Deer, *O.v. clavium* is usually less than 25 kg. The Florida Keys White-tailed Deer was once considered threatened with perhaps only 30 surviving in 1949, but under protection they had recovered to a population of 300–400 by 1980.

White-tailed Deer live in a wide variety of habitats, usually with some cover in which to hide. They browse and graze on a wide variety of vegetable matter, including grass, herbs, fungi, lichen, bark and twigs. By about 1900 its US population had been reduced to about 500,000 but, under protection and management, it has risen to over 12 million, and about 2 million are killed each year by sport hunters. They rarely gather in large herds, but live in small family groups. Males do not form harems or defend territories, but move on once they have mated with a female. After a gestation of about 201 days, twins are usually born (except the first pregnancy which is usually a single young); occasionally there are 3 or 4 young in a litter. For the first month the female leaves the young hidden in dense cover, they start nibbling vegetation when a few days old, can run at about 3 weeks and are weaned by about 4 months. Young males are independent by about 1 year, but females usually remain with the mother for 2 years. Both White-tailed and Black-tailed Deer are often seen in zoos and have lived for up to 20 years in captivity. In some areas they have now increased to such an extent that they are causing damage to the vegetation and are in need of culling.

PUDU

Northern Pudu

There are two species of Pudu: the Northern Pudu *Pudu mephistophiles* which is found in the Andes of north South America from Colombia and Ecuador to northern Peru; and the Chilean or Southern Pudu *P. pudu*, found in southern Chile and south-western Argentina. The pudus are among the world's smallest deer, less than 1 m long, with a shoulder height under 40 cm and a weight of less than 10 kg. Neither species has more than a vestigial tail, and both species have short unbranched antlers. The differences between the species are fairly minimal, the most noticeable being that the hooves of the Northern are narrower and more pointed than those of the southern. They live in forests, thickets and dense grass and range from sea level to the lower hills of the Andes, to altitudes of 4000 m. The Northern Pudu is threatened, mainly due to habitat destruction, but also by hunting, and by burning grass during the dry season. Very little is known of the breeding biology of Pudus in the wild. The does are believed to produce a single fawn, occasionally twins, and they are fully grown at about 3 months, and sexually mature at 1 year. The Chilean Pudu is now being kept in a few zoos, and its breeding population is slowly building up.

The 4 related species of brocket deer *Mazama* spp. found in South America and north to Mexico, are slightly larger. The zoo population of Brocket Deer, consisting mainly of Red Brocket *M. americana* and Brown Brocket *M. gouazoubira*, is fairly small but they are now regularly breeding in small numbers.

ROE DEER *Capreolus capreolus*

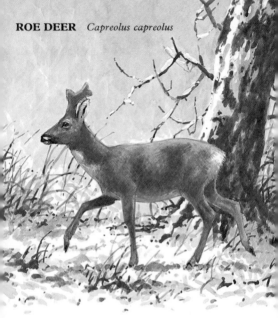

The Roe Deer is found throughout most of Europe, where it is the smallest native deer eastwards through Russia to Siberia. It is absent from Iceland, Ireland and northern Scandinavia. It grows to a maximum length of 41 cm, stands up to 75 cm at the shoulder and weighs up to 50 kg; the largest animals are generally those from Siberia. The males carry short, spiky antlers up to 23 cm long, which rarely have more than three points. Like many other deer, Roe have been introduced by man. In Britain the native Roe Deer died out in much of England and Siberian Roe were introduced into East Anglia. They are mostly found in woodland with thick undergrowth.

They have adapted to agricultural and even suburban areas, hiding by day in small copses and woodlands; Roe Deer are mainly active at night or dusk and dawn. They are mostly browsers, feeding on bushes such as bramble as well as deciduous leaves and shoots, grasses and herbs. The males (bucks) rut in summer and mark their territory by 'fraying' small trees, scraping them with their antlers. The gestation period varies between 5–9½ months and the 1–3 young (usually twins) are left hidden in separate places for the first 10 days after birth, until they accompany the mother. The young stay with the mother until the following year. The young reach sexual maturity at about 16 months, and in the wild they have lived up to 17 years, though 10–12 years is more usual. In captivity, although they breed freely and have been bred through several generations, they are not normally as long lived. Roe Deer are important game animals in Europe, particularly in Germany where about ½-million are killed each year.

OKAPI *Okapia johnstoni*

The Okapi was one of the last large mammals to be discovered by Europeans, although it had long been known to the pygmies of the Congo. In 1900 Sir Harry Johnston (after whom it was named), a British naturalist and the Governor of Uganda, sent two strips of striped skin to the British Museum. Soon after he was able to send two skulls and a skin, and it was then realised that it was closely related to the giraffe. In 1918 the first live Okapi was exhibited in Europe. The Okapi is a forest dwelling giraffe, found only in the Zaire (Congo) River basin. They live alone, in pairs or in small family groups, browsing on leaves, as well as the fruit and seeds, of a wide variety of plants. They are mainly active by day, and use well trodden paths, but disappear into dense undergrowth when alarmed.

Okapis grow to a length of about 2.1 m, a shoulder height of 1.7 m and a weight of 250 kg; the males have small horns covered in hair. Living in dark forests, Okapis have relatively poor eyesight (though their exceptionally long tongue can be used to clean the eyes), but have large ears and acute hearing. The single young is born after a gestation of up to about 490 days, and in captivity an Okapi has lived for over 33 years. A captive female gave birth to 12 young, the last when she had reached an age of 26 years. Okapis now breed regularly in captivity, and most of those in zoos were bred in captivity. Although they are probably fairly rare, they are not thought to be in any immediate danger.

GIRAFFE *Giraffa camelopardalis*

Masai giraffe

The Giraffe once occurred in most of the open country of Africa, but since about AD 600 has been restricted to areas south of the Sahara and in the past 100 years has been exterminated in most of western and southern Africa. Several different colour forms occur within the species. The Giraffe is the tallest living animal and a male grows to a maximum height of 5.3 m, with a shoulder height of up to 3.7 m and a weight of up to 1800 kg, but usually less; females are slightly smaller than males. Because of the enormous length of the neck, and to prevent blood rushing to the head when the giraffe is drinking, there is a series of valves in the blood vessels. Giraffes are browsers, feeding on leaves, buds and shoots, particularly those of acacias. The single young is born after a gestation of about 457 days; it is able to stand about 20 minutes after birth and is soon walking. It is suckled for up to 13 months and remains with its mother for 4–5 months more. Giraffes can run at speeds of over 50 kph and have few enemies other than man, although lion occasionally attack the young. Giraffes are kept in most large zoos where they breed regularly and have lived for over 36 years; the greatest age known in the wild is 26 years.

Rothschild's Giraffe

Reticulated Giraffe

:peckers

PRONGHORN *Antilocapra americana*

Pronghorn were once found widely in North America from Saskatchewan south to northern Mexico, and are still found in scrub, semi-desert and grassland habitats within that range. They grow up to 1.5 m long, a shoulder height of 1 m and a weight of up to 70 kg; males are slightly larger than females. Both sexes carry horns which are unusual in that they consist of a central bone core, similar to that of cattle and sheep, and an outer keratinous (horn) casing which is shed annually. Pronghorns are usually gregarious; young males form bachelor herds, and older males hold territories. The females move about in groups. Fawns (1 at the first birth, thereafter twins) are born in spring after a gestation of about 252 days. They are sexually mature by 15–16 months and in captivity have lived for over 11 years. Outside the breeding season the herds often link up and may form large aggregations of all ages and sexes – up to 1000 have been recorded. These herds sometimes move at speeds of nearly 50 kph and a record of 86.5 kph has been recorded. Before Europeans arrived in America there were an estimated 35 million Pronghorns, which were reduced to about 13,000 by the 1920s. Under protection their numbers have risen to about ½-million, and about 40,000 are killed each year by sport hunters. However, the southern populations are still endangered and the Lower California Pronghorn, *A. americana peninsularis*, is considered endangered; it is restricted to southern Baja California. In the 1920s the population numbered some 500, but by the late 1970s it was down to about 80. The Sonoran Pronghorn *A. a. sonoriensis* from the Sonoran Desert, with a population of less than 450 is also considered endangered. It is not decreasing in the USA, but in Mexico has dropped by over 60 per cent in the last 25 years. A number of American and Canadian zoos have small herds of Pronghorn, but they are rarely seen elsewhere.

NYALA *Tragelaphus angasi*

The Nyala occurs in several widely separated populations in south-eastern Africa from Malawi and Mozambique south to South Africa. It is found mainly in dense thickets, forest and woodland, usually near water. The males, grow to a maximum length of 1.95 m, a shoulder height of 1.2 m and a weight of 140 kg; females are smaller. Only the male has the long spiral horns; the record length is 83.5 cm. Nyala are active by day and night, and in areas where they are hunted are very secretive. They

male

are mainly browsers, feeding on leaves, bark, buds, fruit and also grass. They live in small groups (occasionally in small herds of up to 30 animals) consisting of an old male, several females and their young. The young are born after a gestation of just over 7 months and for the first week or two after birth are left hidden in undergrowth. They reach maturity in their second year. Their only enemies, apart from man, are the larger predators such as leopard, but the young are occasionally killed by birds of prey and even baboons. In captivity Nyala have lived for up to 16 years; most of those in zoos have been captive bred.

female

ELANDS

The 2 closely related species of eland occur only in Africa. The Common Eland *Tragelaphus oryx* was once found throughout Africa, south from Ethiopia and southern Zaire, except in dense forest and arid desert areas, but excessive hunting, combined with the encroachment of agriculture and outbreaks of rinderpest, have eliminated it from much of its range. It grows to a length of 3.45 m, a shoulder height of 1.8 m and a weight of 1 tonne; males are larger than females. Both sexes carry horns, but the male's grow to over 1 m, nearly double the length of the females'. Eland have been domesticated in both Africa and the Soviet Union. They tame easily, provide high quality meat and are capable of living in conditions under which cattle do not thrive. The single calf (occasionally twins) is born

Cape Eland

after a gestation of up to 9 months; females reach sexual maturity at about 3 years, males at 4. In captivity Eland have lived to over 23 years and given birth at 19 years. Large numbers are kept and bred in zoos and further substantial numbers in game ranches and parks in eastern and southern Africa.

The Giant Eland, or Lord Derby's Eland *T. derbianus*, once widespread in a belt running south of the Sahara from Senegal to the southern Sudan, is now divided into well-separated populations. Its scientific name honours the Earl of Derby who introduced eland into his park at Knowsley Hall near Liverpool. The western population of Giant Eland *T.d. gigas*, now confined to a limited area on the borders of Mali, Senegal and Guinea, is considered endangered. There are few Giant Elands in captivity; the only breeding herd is in Pretoria Zoo.

Giant Eland

BONGO *Tragelaphus euryceros*

The forest-dwelling Bongo remained one of the least-known antelopes until the present century. It is confined to high forests in West Africa (Sierra Leone, Liberia, Ivory Coast, Cameroun, Ghana and Togo) and also the Zaire River Basin and the forests of Kenya and southern Ethiopia. Over most of its range it is a lowland species, but in Kenya, occurs at

altitudes of 2000–3000 m. It grows to about 2.5 m long, 1.4 m at the shoulder and weighs up to 220 kg, both sexes have spiral horns which may be up to 1 m long. The females are usually more brightly coloured, and old males may be very dark. Bongos are normally solitary or live in pairs, or occasionally gather in small groups consisting of females and their young. They usually live near water, and wallow in mud holes. When alarmed they charge through dense undergrowth with the horns laid back over their shoulders, in older animals this produces bare patches in the fur on their back. Bongos eat a wide variety of vegetation, but are mainly browsers eating bamboo, cassava, and sweet potato, and sometimes raiding farms for plants such as coco yams. When browsing on trees they often stand on their hind legs to reach 2.5 m or more, and they may use their horns to dig for roots. They often seek out saltlicks, where small groups of Bongos may congregate. The single young is normally born in December or January, after a gestation of about 284 days. For the first few days after birth the young are left hidden in dense undergrowth. Their main enemy, other than man is the Leopard, and when cornered by hunters adult Bongos will defend themselves. Calves are also preyed on by Golden Cats and Pythons. Bongos are not particularly numerous in captivity, and until fairly recently were quite rare in zoos. However, they are now breeding regularly and have lived for over 19 years in captivity.

KUDUS

The Greater Kudu *Tragelephus strepsiceros* is found in open savannah country from Chad and Ethiopia south to northern South Africa. Hunted to extinction in many parts of its range, it has been widely reintroduced in South Africa. It grows to a length of up to 2.45 m, a shoulder height of 1.5 m and weight of 270 kg; males are slightly larger than females. Normally only males have horns, which grow to about 1 m long, the record being over 1.8 m. Mainly browsers, they feed on bushes and trees, particularly acacias, occasionally on grasses. They live in rather open woodlands, with thickets in which to hide, in small groups which consist of females and their young accompanied by one or two males. Renowned for their leaping ability, the clear 2.5 m with ease. Greater Kudu make a variety of noises – the females and young males have a *moo* and the young a *maaa*, the males a quiet snorting *humph*. They can be seen in most larger zoos. In captivity they breed freely and have lived for over 20 years.

The Lesser Kudu *T. imberbis* is found in East Africa, from Ethiopia and Somalia south to Kenya and Tanzania, living in dense vegetation. Smaller than the Greater, it grows to 1.4 m long, a shoulder height of 1 m and a maximum weight of 105 kg. The male's horns are up to 90 cm long. They are good leapers: leaps of 9.2 m long have been recorded.

Greater and Lesser Kudu horns

BUSHBUCK *Tragelephus scriptus*

The Bushbuck or Harnessed Antelope is found over most of Africa, south of the Sahara and Ethiopia to the Transvaal and Cape, but absent from most of the western side of southern Africa. Bushbuck grow to a length of up to 1.5 m, plus a tail of about 25 cm, stand just over 1 m at the shoulder and weigh about 50 kg. The horns grow to about 40 cm, the record being

57 cm; females do not normally carry horns. They occur in dense thickets, woodlands and forest with thick undergrowth at altitudes of up to 4000 m (13,000 ft). They often use tunnels and well worn tracks through the dense undergrowth and are usually found close to water. They browse on shoots, leaves and buds as well as grazing on grasses and herbs. Bushbuck are mostly active in the early morning or late afternoon, but are also active on moonlit nights, or during the day when it is overcast. However, where they are hunted they are mainly nocturnal. They normally live singly with both sexes living in relatively small areas of 15–30 ha: in some areas they migrate in search of food. They breed throughout the year, and a single calf is born after a gestation of about 6 months. For the first few weeks after birth the calf remains concealed in dense vegetation and is only visited occasionally by the mother to allow it to suckle; they are weaned at 6 months and reach sexual maturity at about 1 year. Bushbuck are prey to a wide variety of animals, particularly when young; their principal enemies are leopards and crocodiles and, when young, other cats and pythons. In captivity Bushbuck have lived for 12 years. They are not common in zoos, but are bred in small numbers.

SITATUNGA *Tragelephus spekei*

The Sitatunga is a semi-aquatic antelope with elongated hooves adapted to walking on marshy and swampy ground. Its Latin name is in honour of John Speke, the discoverer of the source of the Nile. The Sitatunga is found in swampy habitats in central Africa as far south as Botswana, and also around Lake Chad, and a few other isolated areas. Its range is very fragmented and in many areas it is endangered or extinct. The males, which are slightly larger than the female, grow to a length of 1.7 m, a shoulder height of 1.25 m and a maximum weight of 120 kg. The horns of the male grow to a maximum of 92 cm. Sitatungas

spend most of their life in or near water, in dense reed beds or papyrus swamps. They swim well and often completely submerge to avoid danger or when feeding; they graze on reeds, sedges and other aquatic vegetation, and also meadow grasses and occasionally crops on nearby farms. They breed throughout the year, and the single young (occasionally twins) is born after a gestation of about 247 days, on high dry ground (in emergency the female apparently builds a platform of trodden vegetation), where the young remain for about a month. The females are mature at about 1 year, the males at about 18 months. Their main predators are crocodiles, Leopards, large snakes and on dry ground, Lions. Sitatungas are kept in many of the larger zoos, where they breed freely.

NILGAI *Boselaphus tragocamelus*

male

The Nilgai or Blue Bull is a large, rather ungainly antelope found in eastern Pakistan and India. It grows to about 2.1 m long and stands about 1.5 m, with a 50 cm tail; weighing up to 270 kg; males are larger than females. Both sexes have a short mane, and the males have a throat tuft, and short cone-like horns (the record is under 30 cm). Nilgai are mostly found in sparsely wooded hills, open scrub and plains and even cultivated areas, where they may damage crops. They appear to breed throughout the year, though most calves are born June–October, after a gestation of up to 277 days. There are usually twins, or sometimes a single young. The Nilgai is often fairly abundant in India, and shows little fear of man. This is probably due to the fact that it is not normally persecuted; its horns are small and not sought after as trophies, its meat is allegedly poor tasting and being closely related and similar to the cow, in Hindu areas it is completely free from molestation. They can go for long periods without water and only seek shade during the hottest parts of the day. They are both browsers and grazers and are often attracted by fallen fruit and by the flowers of the Mohwa (Mahua) tree, *Manilkara* spp., which are also used by Hindus for making sacred garlands. Nilgai tame easily and thrive in captivity, where they breed freely and have lived for over 21 years.

female

ASIATIC WATER BUFFALO
Bubalus arnee (= bubalis)

The Asiatic Water Buffalo found in India is the wild ancestor of the domestic Water Buffalo which has been widely introduced elsewhere by man. In the wild the Water Buffalo is usually found in wet meadows, swamps, and overgrown river valleys where they feed on the lush vegetation at the water's edge. They wallow in water and mud in order to form a protective cake of mud through which insects cannot penetrate. First domesticated nearly 5000 years ago, it has been estimated that Water Buffalo now number 75 million worldwide, mostly in India and south-east Asia. Domesticated Wild Buffalo are also found in southern Europe, the Middle East, north and east Africa, Madagascar, Central and South America, Australia and many other parts of the world; and there are now feral populations also living in many of these areas. They are primarily beasts of burden and used for ploughing and tilling rice paddies. They also produce rich milk and excellent leather and become extremely tame. The Wild Asiatic Water Buffalo grows to a length of up to 3 m, with a shoulder height of 1.9 m and a tail of up to 1 m; they weigh up to 1200 kg and their horns have a spread of up to 1.2 m. Although such a widespread and common domestic species, the Asiatic Water Buffalo is comparatively rare in zoos and is threatened in the wild.

LOWLAND ANOA *Bubalus depressicornis*

The Lowland Anoa is a small buffalo, closely related to the Asiatic water buffalo, found only in the lowland forests of the Celebes (Sulawesi). It grows to about 1.7 m long, plus a tail of 30 cm and stands about 1 m at the shoulder. Both sexes carry horns which grow up to 37 cm. Anoas are mainly dirunal feeding in the morning mostly on grasses, cane shoots and water plants. They live singly or in pairs and are extremely shy and wary. A single calf is born after a gestation of up to 315 days, and in captivity have lived up to 28 years. Only a small number are in zoos, but most have been bred in captivity. In the wild their future is far from secure and they are endangered. The main threats are from habitat destruction, but also from hunting.

In the highland forests of the Celebes a close relative of the Lowland Anoa occurs, it is the Highland Anoa B. quarlesi which is slightly smaller, has less clearly defined markings and is more hairy, but in other respects it is similar and is also endangered. Only a few are kept in zoos, but some are being bred. Another close relative of the Anoa is the Tamaraw Bubalus mindorensis which is one of the rarest animals in the world, with under 200 of them surviving in the forests and swamps of Mindoro in the Philippines. At the time of writing there are none in captivity, but since they are related to Buffalo it is likely that they would flourish in captivity. Their rarity is due to loss of habitat plus hunting by people and also from diseases caught from domestic cattle.

GAUR OR SELADANG *Bos gaurus*

The Gaur, the largest of the wild cattle, is found in forested areas from Nepal and India east to Indochina, and south to peninsular Malaya. It grows to a length of up to 3.3 m plus a tail of 1 m, is up to 2.2 m at the shoulder, and weighs up to 1 tonne; males are larger than females and carry the longer horns, the longest being nearly 120 cm long, and over 50 cm around the base. Gaur live in and around clearings in forested hills, up to an altitude of 1800 m (5900 ft), usually near to water. They are mainly grazers, feeding on grasses, but also browse on forest trees and sometimes emerge from the forest to feed on maize and other crops. They live in groups of up to 40 led by a single mature bull. A single calf is born after a gestation of up to 280 days, which suckles for 9 months, and reaches maturity at 2–3 years, but males probably wait longer before mating; one has lived over 20 years in captivity. The Gaur is threatened by the destruction of the forests, as well as by hunting, and they have also suffered from diseases transmitted by domestic cattle. The Gaur is the ancester of the domestic Gayal or Mithan. Gayal sometimes occur in a feral state in the forests.

The rarest of the wild cattle is the Kouprey *Bos sauveli* which was first discovered in 1937 in Cambodia close to the border of Thailand, Laos and Vietnam. Unfortunately the area where it lives has long been a war zone, and although it has been sighted intermittently its future in the wild is very insecure. Although it was exhibited in Paris Zoo none are in captivity at the time of writing.

Domestic Gayal

BANTENG *Bos javanicus*

The Banteng – known as the Tsaine in Burma and Sapiutan in Malaya – is found in south-east Asia from India and Burma, Thailand and Indochina south through peninsular Malaya to Java and Borneo. In the Sunda Islands, Bali, Java and eastern India Banteng have been domesticated, and they hybridise freely with humped zebu cattle of southern Asia. The wild Banteng grows to a length of up to 2.25 m plus a tail of 70 cm, stands 1.6 m at the shoulder and weighs up to 900 kg; males are larger than the females and carry horns up to about 60 cm long (occasionally longer). Unlike the Gaur, which is usually found in hill country, the Banteng prefers more open flat country with glades of grass or bamboo except where they have been forced to retreat into the forests with the advance of agriculture into their preferred habitat. They feed mainly on grasses, bamboos and the shoots and leaves of trees and bushes. They often

visit areas where the undergrowth has been burnt, allowing fresh green grass to grow after the rains. They live in groups of up to about 40, led by a single mature bull, the other males living in bachelor herds or singly. They breed during most months of the year and 1–2 calves are born after a gestation of up to 10 months. They are suckled for about 9 months, and mature at about 2 years. Throughout most of their range Banteng have declined and, in addition to the threats posed by habitat loss and hunting, they are subject to diseases of domestic cattle and hybridisation with domestic cattle which may effectively 'swamp' them. The Banteng is probably the closest living wild relative of the extinct Aurochs, which was the wild ancestor of the domestic cattle and oxen of Europe. Aurochsen became extinct in 1627 when the last one was killed in Poland, but a reconstructed animal has been bred in Munich Zoo by cross breeding primitive cattle.

female

WILD YAK *Bos mutus*

The Yak is one of the smaller species of cattle and is found at altitudes of up to 6100 m (20,000 ft) in the bleak steppes close to the snow-line in the Tibetan plateau, north of the Himalayas. They grow to a length of 3.2 m, stand up to 2 m at the shoulder and weigh up to 1 tonne; females are considerably smaller than males and the horns of the bull may be up to 75 cm long. The Yak is insulated against the extreme cold of its environment by the fringes of shaggy hair beneath which there is a dense under fur of soft, matted hair, which is shed in large patches in spring. The Yak has been domesticated; the domesticated animals do not have such massive horns as Wild Yaks, and often have some white markings, particularly on the chest and tail. Yak live in small herds, which may congregate in spring when fresh grass attracts them. The rut is in autumn and a single calf is born in alternate years in June, after a gestation of 9 months. Calves become independent when they are about 1 year old, but do not reach full size until over 6 years old; they have lived up to 25 years. Like the ancestors of most other domestic animals, the Wild Yak is increasingly rare in its native habitat; although protected they are still hunted. The Domestic Yak is well-adapted to life at altitudes over 2000 m (6500 ft). It serves as a beast of burden, its wool and hair, which is very strong, is used in making rugs, and produces a very rich milk. Its meat is eaten and its leather used in making clothes and other articles.

AFRICAN BUFFALO *Synceros caffer*

The African Buffalo is found in a wide variety of habitats but generally includes open grass and dense cover, often close to water. At one time it was found over most of Africa, south of the Sahara, but due to overhunting and spreading agriculture its range is now considerably fragmented, and most populations are reduced. The African Buffalo grows to a length of up to 3 m, plus a tail of just over 1 m, stands up to 1.7 m at the shoulder and weighs up to 900 kg. However, there is considerable geographical variation in size, and those found in the tropical forests are about half the size of those from the savannahs. Both sexes carry horns, which in the males are massive on the top of the head. Buffalo were renowned among the big game hunters as one of the most dangerous of all animals when wounded or cornered, although they appear to be more docile than generally believed. They live in herds which can number up to 1500, but are usually around 300–400, in open plains areas or around 20 in forests. African Buffalo breed at most times of the year, and a single calf is born after a gestation of about 11 months. The male calves leave the mother when they are about 2 years old and join bachelor herds, but young females remain with the mother until they are about 4 years old and sexually mature. African Buffalo are exhibited in most of the larger zoos and are regularly bred; they have lived nearly 30 years in captivity. Although still relatively abundant in parts of East Africa, the African Buffalo is more or less extinct outside parks and protected areas in South Africa, and increasingly rare in west Africa.

AMERICAN BISON *Bison bison*

The American Bison, also known in North America
as the Buffalo, although it is not a true Buffalo (see p.
334), was once one of the most abundant large
mammals on the entire continent, with an estimated
50 million ranging from Alaska to Mexico. The
American Bison can grow to a length of up to 3.5 m
long, with a tail of about 50 cm, stands about 2.5 m at
the shoulder and can weigh over a tonne, but most are
smaller. When the first European colonists arrived in
North America the destruction of the enormous
herds of Bison started almost immediately, and they
were hunted both for meat and hides. Many Indian
tribes were almost totally dependant on the Bison; in
addition to providing meat, their hides provided
clothing, footwear and tents, and other parts of the
animal such as sinews and bones supplied
bowstrings, needles and other artifacts. During the
wars against the Indians, Bison were killed to help
subdue them, and the Bison were also eliminated as
competitors for grazing, and to clear the land for corn
growing on the prairies. The spread of the railroads
westwards accelerated the demise of the Bison, with
travellers shooting from trains and leaving the car-
cases to rot, and others hunted them merely for their
tongues – which were a delicacy. By 1890 the
destruction of the Bison was almost complete and less
than 1000 survived in the whole of North America.
Fortunately the pioneer American conservationist,
William Hornaday, led a campaign to save them

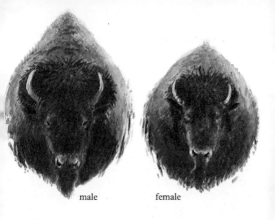

male   female

and today there are over 50,000. The Yellowstone National Park is the only place in the USA in which Bison have lived continuously, but they have now been widely reintroduced into their former range. A separate subspecies, the Wood Bison *Bison bison athabascae*, occurs in the northern parts of its range, but most populations have mixed blood – even in Yellowstone. In the 1920s Plains Buffalo were introduced into the Wood Buffalo National Park in Canada, in order to boost the population; fortunately in 1957 about 200 pure bred Wood Bison were found in an isolated part of the park cut off from the rest. American Bison are kept in many zoos, and even on private ranches in America, and have been hybridised with cattle.

EUROPEAN BISON *Bison bonasus*

Like the American Bison, the European Bison or Wisent, was once widespread and abundant. However, its disappearance from most of its range was centuries ago, in prehistoric times. Like the American species, the European Bison occurred in both woodlands and in open grassy plains – though in recent history it was most found in woodlands and forests. It grows to a length of about 2.5 m, plus a tail

338

of up to 50 cm, stands just under 2 m at the shoulder, and weighs up to 1 tonne (but usually less). European Bison normally give birth to a single calf after a gestation of 9 months. The calf is weaned at about 7 months, but stays with the mother until the next calf is born; they have lived over 20 years in the wild.

European Bison sometimes graze on grasses in forest clearings but are primarily browsers on leaves and shoots of deciduous trees; they also eat acorns in autumn. By the 1920s the European Bison was totally extinct in the wild. Earlier this century 2 fragments of its populations had survived in Lithuania (the last of which died in 1921) and in the Caucasus (the last of which died in 1925). Fortunately there were a number of animals in captivity and a captive herd was established in Poland in an enclosure in the Bialowieza Forest, where over 700 Bison were living before World War I, although they were all dead by 1919. The new captive herd gradually increased, and was subsequently released into the forest, where they still flourish; animals from this herd have been reintroduced, under semi-natural conditions, in other reserves in Poland, USSR and Romania, as well as being found in many zoos.

The ancestor of domestic cattle, also related to the Bison, is the Aurochs or Urus; it was once found in the forests of Europe but as a result of man's hunting activities became extinct in Britain by the tenth century AD, and the last one was killed in Poland in the seventeenth century.

FOREST DUIKERS

Grey Duiker

Common Duiker

Yellow-backed
Duiker

There are about 16 species of forest duikers found throughout Africa, south of the Sahara. They are all rather hunch-backed and small – less than 1.5 m long and under 80 cm at the shoulder. They live in a wide variety of habitats, including dense forest and scrub and open savannah. Although they are often relatively abundant they are rarely seen, as they are mainly nocturnal and keep well hidden. In some parts of Africa they are important sources of meat and in West Africa some species have been tamed. Among the species most commonly seen in captivity are Maxwell's Duiker *Cephalophus maxwelli* which is a common species found in West Africa from Senegal to Nigeria; it is fairly small, only growing to a shoulder height of 40 cm; the Yellow-backed Duiker *C. sylvicultor* although widely distributed from Senegal to Kenya and south to Angola and Zambia, is rare within that range; it is kept in a few zoos and is the largest species of duiker, growing to a shoulder height of 80 cm and weighing up to 64 kg. One of the most attractive duikers, which is kept in a few zoos is the Banded or Zebra Duiker *C. zebra* which occurs from Sierra Leone to the Ivory Coast; its name is derived from its attractively striped back. Little is known about the breeding habits of most duikers but Maxwell's Duiker gives birth to a single young after a gestation of 120 days; it starts to eat leaves at about 2 weeks and is weaned about 2 months later. Many duikers are locally threatened and one of the rarest species is probably Jentink's Duiker *C. jentinki* which probably only numbers a few hundred.

COMMON OR DEFASSA WATERBUCK
Kobus ellipsiprymnus

Common Waterbuck male

The Waterbuck is widespread in wooded areas with access to water, over much of Africa south of the Sahara. Several subspecies have been described, based mainly on differences in colour and rump pattern. The males, which are only slightly larger than the females, are up to 2.2 m long, 1.3 m at the shoulder, and weigh up to 250 kg. The male's horns grow to nearly 1 m. Waterbuck feed mainly on grass, together with leaves of bushes and trees. The males hold territories, which include access to water, and although bachelor groups are allowed to wander across the territories, as are females, they are defended against other mature males. The single young is born after a gestation of about 280 days and is suckled for about 6 months, and reaches sexual maturity after about 13–14 months. Both the subspecies illustrated are commonly exhibited in zoos, and have lived for up to 18 years.

In addition to the Common Waterbuck several other closely related species are exhibited in zoos, such as the Lechwe (see p. 346) and the Nile Lechwe *K. megaceros*.

Defassa Waterbuck female

KOB   *Kobus kob*

The Kob is widespread in the African savannahs from south of the Sahara from Senegal to western Kenya. It grows to a length of up to 1.8 m, plus a tail of up to 40 cm, stands up to 1 m at the shoulder and weighs up to 120 kg; the females are smaller than males. Both sexes carry horns which in the male grow to around 40 cm, the record being nearly 70 cm. Kob live in herds of up to about 40 females, occasionally more, together with one or more mature males; the immature males forming bachelor herds. They are active mainly in the early morning and late afternoon,

grazing on grasses and herbage, and occasionally browsing on shrubs and bushes; they travel to water to drink each day. They breed throughout the year. In areas of high population density the males form territories during the breeding season. These territories or 'leks' are usually higher than the surrounding countryside and are often used for many years. A single calf is born after a gestation of up to 9 months, and is active soon after birth, following its mother. The young are suckled for about 6 months and are mature at 2 years, but males do not join the rut until 3–4 years old. Kob are preyed upon by Lion, Leopard, hyenas and Hunting Dogs.

A closely related, but smaller species, the Puku *K. vardoni* occurs in the Savannahs of Zaire, Tanzania and south to Angola and northern Botswana.

dark form, *Kobus kob leucotis*

LECHWE *Kobus leche*

The Lechwe occurs in 3 fairly distinctive subspecies:
the Black Lechwe *Kobus leche smithemani,* found in
northern Zambia; the Red or Zambesi Lechwe *K.l.
leche,* found from Upper Zambezi and Victoria Falls
to the Lower Zambesi and Okavanga; and the Brown
or Kafue Lechwe *K.l. kafuensis* in Kafue Zambia.
The Kawambwa Lechwe *K.l. robertsi,* which used to

occur in northern Zambia, is extinct. Many of the populations of Lechwe are reduced and several already extinct; others are threatened and the species is classified as vulnerable. Male Lechwe, which are on average larger than females, grow to a maximum of 1.8 m long, a shoulder height of 1.1 m and a weight of 130 kg, though are usually lighter. The males' horns are long, growing up to 1 m. Lechwe are normally found close to water, in floodplains, marshes, swamps and the edges of lakes, feeding on grasses and other vegetation from the water's edge to 50 cm deep. In shallow water they progress in a series of bounding leaps, but are also good swimmers. The social structure of Lechwe is very variable and complex. They live in groups which may vary from small parties to herds of several thousand; on the Kafue floodplain, where there is an abundance of food, they may congregate in dense herds of as many as 200 per km². The breeding behaviour of the males is particularly interesting: the species has a 'lek' breeding system – clusters of small territories, anything up to 200 in number, are each occupied by a male, through them large herds of females wander at will. Most births occur from July to September, after a gestation of about 8 months. The single young is weaned after about 6 months and females start breeding when about 1 year old, but the males take no part in breeding until about 4 years old. The Lechwe is exhibited in many zoos, and most have been bred in captivity; they have lived for up to 15 years.

ROAN ANTELOPE *Hippotragus equinus*

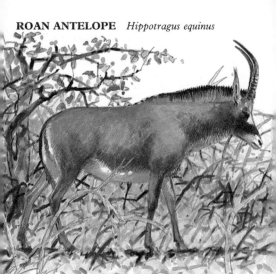

The Roan Antelope is widespread in Africa south of
the Sahara, although it has been exterminated from
much of its range, giving a highly fragmented
distribution; in many areas it is endangered. It has
been translocated and introduced into a number of
areas, particularly in South Africa. The Roan Antelope is similar to the Sable, but slightly larger. The
males (which are larger than the females), grow to a
length of up to 2.65 m, shoulder height of 1.6 m, and a

weight of up to 300 kg. Both sexes carry horns, which in the male grow to 1 m. Roan Antelope live in open woodland and gallery forest, close to water; they normally live in small groups, of up to 15, comprising females and their young, led by an old male. These herds may join with others during the dry season, and may also associate with other antelope, Zebras, Ostriches etc. The single calf is born after a gestation of up to 286 days, and matures at 2½–3 years. Roan Antelope are not particularly common in zoos, but can be seen in many of the larger collections and are now being bred irregularly. In addition to being extensively hunted, Roan Antelope have been slaughtered as part of Tse-tse Fly control programmes, and have also lost large parts of their range through agricultural encroachment.

The related Blaauwbok or Bluebuck (*H. leucophaeus*) was formerly found in the southern tip of Africa, but was exterminated by the early European settlers, by about AD 1800.

SABLE ANTELOPE
Hippotragus niger

The Sable Antelope was formerly widespread in Southern Africa, from southern Kenya and south-eastern Zaire, south to the Orange Free State and Transvaal. Its range is now considerably reduced, mainly due to hunting by man, and it is extinct in most of South Africa; it has been re-introduced into

Swaziland and other parts of South Africa. There are 3 subspecies, the rarest of which is the Giant Sable which occurs in Angola. The Sable grows to a length of 2.5 m, a shoulder height of 1.4 m and a weight of 270 kg; both sexes have horns and those of the male grow to a maximum of 65 cm. Sable Antelope inhabit thick bush country and live in herds of up to 100 individuals, mostly females and young dominated by an adult male. The young males, of 22 years or more, form bachelor herds, in which dominance is established by fighting. When the males are about 5–6 years old they become solitary and try to establish dominance over groups of females. The single calf is born after a gestation of up to 281 days, and remains hidden for about 10 days. Sable Antelopes are exhibited in many of the larger zoos, although there do not appear to be any Giant Sable in captivity; one has lived for over 19 years in captivity.

ORYX

Scimitar-horned Oryx

Gemsbok

There are 2 species of oryx both found in Africa. All oryx are gregarious, living in herds, which may number thousands, particularly when rains appear after a prolonged drought.

The Gemsbok *Oryx gazella* is found in open arid habitats in eastern Africa from Ethiopia and Somalia southwards (where it is usually known as the Beisa Oryx *O. gazella beisa* or Fringe-eared Oryx *O. gazella callotis*, and in Southern Africa. Over much of its range, particularly in the southeast it is now extinct, but in Namibia and Botswana it is still abundant. It grows to a length of up to 2.35 m, plus a tail of up to 90 cm, stands 1.4 m at the shoulder and can weigh over 200 kg. Both sexes carry horns which can grow to 1.5 m long. All 3 subspecies of Gemsbok are to be seen in zoos, and safari parks where they breed freely. They have also been kept on ranches in south and east Africa and many biologists believe that they are more productive than cattle in arid habitats.

The smaller Scimitar-horned Oryx *Oryx dammah* was once found in most of the areas in and around the Sahara, except where total desert conditions prevailed, a range much of which it shared with the Addax (p. 356). In recent years it has been exterminated from all but a few localities. Although on the brink of extinction in the wild it is thriving in captivity, and several zoos breed substantial numbers. International co-operation among zoos should ensure that, should suitable areas become available, they could be re-introduced into the wild.

WHITE OR ARABIAN ORYX *Oryx leucoryx*

The story of the Arabian Oryx is one of the success stories of captive breeding in zoos, as a handful of zoos got together with the Fauna Preservation Society to save it from extinction. It grows to a length of 1 m plus a tail of 30 cm, and stands 90 cm at the shoulder and weighs up to 50 kg; the horns, carried by both sexes, grow to 70 cm in the males. It is extremely well adapted to desert life, and can survive without drinking water, utilising the moisture in vegetation and dew. In most aspects of its reproduction it is similar to other oryx. The Arabian Oryx was found throughout the arid areas of Arabia, but with the advent of motorised transport and modern rifles, after World War II it was soon reduced to the brink of extinction. In 1962 the Fauna Preservation Society launched Operation Oryx as a result of which three of the last live wild Oryx were captured. These, together with Oryx gathered from a number of zoos and private collections were taken to the USA and formed the nucleus of a world herd. By 20 years later the numbers had built up, new herds had been started in other zoos, animals had also been taken back to the Middle East and 3 re-introduction programmes started in Jordan, Israel and Oman. The latter was close to the site of the original capture, and by the time they were released it was thought that the Arabian Oryx was totally extinct – the last ones being found dead in 1972. In addition to the Arabian Oryx in American and European zoos there are also many in private zoos in Arabia. The Arabian Oryx is said to be the origin of the legends about unicorns; this is possibly because in Roman times young Oryx sometimes had their horns bound together so that they grew together to look like a single horn, and they were then shown in the games and other Roman menageries.

ADDAX *Addax nasomaculatus*

The Addax was once widespread and abundant in the desert and semi-desert areas of North Africa from Mauretania, in the west, to Egypt and the Sudan, in the east. It has been totally eliminated from all but a few scattered localities, mainly in Chad and Niger, and the wild population is probably now in the low hundreds, there may be more in captivity than in the wild. The Addax is rather heavily built and easily exhausted, and consequently easily outrun by mounted hunters armed with modern guns. The Addax grows to a length of 1.7 m, shoulder height of 1.15 m and a weight of up to 125 kg; both sexes carry horns, which in the male may measure over 1 m long. Like the Scimitar-horned Oryx, with which they sometimes associate, they are extremely well adapted to living in arid environments, and can survive without drinking water, utilising moisture in vegetation and dew, and by metabolising body fat. The single young is born after a gestation of up to 264 days, and follows the mother from a few hours after birth; the females are mature at about 2½ years and males at about 2 years. By 1981 there were over 400 in captivity, in most of the world's major zoos, and most of these were bred in captivity, some for several generations. Addax have lived for more than 25 years in captivity.

WILDEBEEST

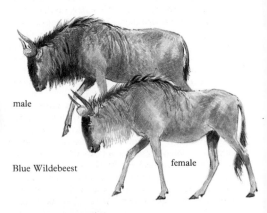

male

Blue Wildebeest

female

Black Wildebeest

There are 2 species of wildebeest or gnu: the Blue Wildebeest or Brindled Gnu *Connochaetes taurinus* is found in open grassland, plains and savannahs in Eastern and Southern Africa. Within historic times its range was much greater, but it has been exterminated in many areas. The Blue Wildebeest grows to a length of up to 2.4 m, stands up to 1.45 m at the shoulder, has a tail of up to 1 m and weighs up to 290 kg; males are slightly larger than females and have horns up to 83 cm long.

The Black Wildebeest *C. gnou* was once widespread in the veldt and plains of southern Africa, but exterminated in the wild during the nineteenth century. Fortunately small populations were saved on private farms, government reserves, and zoos. The Black Wildebeest is slightly smaller than the Blue. Gnus are an important prey for many carnivores, including Lion, Leopard and Hyena; scavengers will feed on the remains of kills. They also suffer from outbreaks of rinderpest, and when migrating large numbers often drown while crossing rivers, or get trampled to death. A single calf is born after a gestation of about 8½ months; within a particular herd most of the births usually occur within short periods of 2–3 weeks and females defend the young against jackals and hyenas. Within a few minutes of birth the calf is able to follow the mother. Gnus become independent at about 1 year old and the males are driven away and join bachelor herds. In the wild they have lived 18 years, in captivity over 21 years.

HARTEBEESTS

The Hartebeest *Alcelaphus buselaphus* occurs in 12 subspecies which differ in horn shape and colouring, and are often known by separate names. They are found in open plains areas of Africa, south of the Sahara, though they formerly occurred in North Africa and Arabia and were tamed in Ancient Egypt. The North African subspecies *A.b. buselaphus* became extinct by the 1920s. Several other subspecies are endangered or threatened, notably Swayne's Hartebeest *A.b. swaynei* from Ethiopia. The closely related Lichtenstein's Hartebeest *A. lichtensteini*, from southern Africa, has also suffered numerous local extinctions. Hartebeest grow to a length of 2.45 m, a shoulder height of 1.45 m and a weight of

Kongoni or Coke's Hartebeest *A. buselaphus cokii* from Kenya and Tanzania

200 kg; males are generally larger than females, and have larger, heavier horns, which grow to 70 cm. Their relatively tall forequarters make Hartebeest look rather ungainly, but they can gallop at up to 80 kph. They are gregarious, often living in large herds; that in Serengeti has been estimated at 18,000, mostly in groups of 300 or more, which occasionally join together to form even larger groups of several thousand. Hartebeest are markedly seasonal in their breeding, but the season varies throughout Africa. The single calf (rarely twins) is born after 8 months gestation, and weaned at about 4 months. Hartebeest are exhibited in many of the world's major zoos, the usual subspecies being the Cape Hartebeest *A.b. caama*, they have lived up to 19 years in captivity.

Lichtenstein's Hartebeest

BONTEBOK AND BLESBOK
Damaliscus dorcas

The common names refer to 2 distinctive subspecies. Both are antelopes of the open grasslands (veldt) of South Africa and were hunted to the brink of extinction as the European colonists spread. The Bontebok *D.d. dorcas* was near to extinction by the 1860s but a few were preserved by Afrikaner families on their farms; however by 1931 they were down to a total of only 17 animals. Since then its numbers have rebuilt and it is now established on many South African private farms and ranches and on Government reserves, where it is increasing and no longer endangered. The Blesbok *D.d. phillipsi* became completely extinct in the wild but is also thriving on farms and ranches and is no longer endangered. The Bontebok National Park was declared in 1931, but has the distinction of being the only National Park to have moved! In 1960 the site of the park was changed to a more favourable habitat. Males of both subspecies are slightly larger than females, standing up to 1 m at the shoulder, up to 1.6 m long and weighing up to 80 kg; the males horns are up to 50 cm

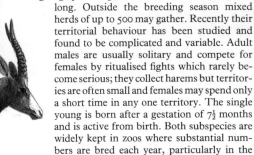

long. Outside the breeding season mixed herds of up to 500 may gather. Recently their territorial behaviour has been studied and found to be complicated and variable. Adult males are usually solitary and compete for females by ritualised fights which rarely become serious; they collect harems but territories are often small and females may spend only a short time in any one territory. The single young is born after a gestation of 7½ months and is active from birth. Both subspecies are widely kept in zoos where substantial numbers are bred each year, particularly in the USA. In captivity Bontebok have lived for over 21 years.

TOPI *Damaliscus lunatus*

The Topi is found in suitable habitat in numerous isolated populations in Africa, south of the Sahara, from Mali to Ethiopia and south to South Africa. It lives in open woodlands and floodplains, and congregates in large herds. Topi are superficially similar to the Hartebeest, having the back sloping towards the hindquarters. They grow to a length of 2 m, a shoulder height of 1.3 m and a weight of 160 kg; both sexes carry horns, those of the male growing to 72 cm. There is considerable variation in the body colour and horn shape of the Topi, and the 8 or so subspecies also have different vernacular names. The Western Korrigum (*D. lunatus korrigum*) is found in West Africa, the Cameroun Korrigum (*D. lunatus purpurescens*) in Nigeria and Cameroun, the Shari Korrigum (*D. lunatus lyra*) in the upper Shari Region, the Tiang (*D. lunatus tiang*) in the Sudan and adjacent Ethiopia, the Topi (*D. lunatus topi*) coastal East Africa and the Jimela (*D. lunatus jimela*) around Lake Victoria and eastern Zaire, Zambia south to Botswana and Transvaal (Kruger National Park). They are found in grasslands, sometimes with open woodland. In some areas male Topi have been shown to have very large territories – up to 100 ha in Rwanda and 200–400 ha in South Africa – and they maintain harems of up to 20 females and their offspring. The breeding season varies throughout Africa and the single calf is born after a gestation of $7\frac{1}{2}$–8 months, and reaches sexual maturity at 2–3 years. They eat grass and herbage and can survive for 4 weeks without drinking. In captivity they have lived for 9 years, but are rarely seen in zoos.

Hunter's Hartebeest *D. hunteri* is closely related to the Topi and occasionally seen in zoos. In the wild it occurs in eastern Kenya, and was once threatened but its numbers have rebuilt again; it was introduced into Tsavo National Park in 1963.

DIK-DIKS

Salt's Dik-dik

Dik-diks are among the smallest antelopes. (The smallest antelopes are the Royal Antelope, which is rarely exhibited in zoos, and the Suni which is also uncommon). There are four species of Dik-dik and Kirk's *Madoqua kirki* is the most widespread and the species most likely to be seen in a zoo. It is found in two populations: from southern Somalia to Tanzania and from Angola to Namibia. It is not much larger than a hare, growing to a length of 55 cm, a shoulder height of 45 cm and a maximum weight of 6.5 kg.

Only the males have horns, which grow to about 11 cm. Dik-diks live in dry, stony, rocky country with low scrubby bushes. Their name is derived from the alarm call they make when startled. Dik-diks browse on low bushes, living in pairs and maintaining territories. The females give birth to 2 single young each year after a gestation of up to 174 days. Dik-diks are extensively hunted, both for meat and skins, and their tiny horns, strung into necklaces, are also sold as souvenirs to tourists. They are preyed on by a wide range of predators ranging in size from large lizards to Leopards and eagles. Kirk's is the only species normally seen in zoos, although others are occasionally exhibited. Guenther's Dik-dik (*Madoqua guentheri*) is found in East Africa; Salt's Dik-dik (*M. saltiana*) in Ethiopia and Somalia; and a fourth, little-known species *M. piacentinii* is found in Somalia.

fawn of Kirk's Dik-dik

IMPALA
Aepyceros melampus

male

The Impala is found in eastern and southern Africa in open woodland, plains, savannahs and in forest clearings. It has been introduced into many ranches in South Africa, outside its original range and in the

USA. Impala grow to a length of 1.5 m, with a 40 cm tail, stand 1 m at the shoulder and weigh up to 65 kg; males are larger than females, and carry horns which are up to 90 cm long. When Impala are alarmed they can make spectacular leaps, up to 3 m high and 10 m long, and they can run at 60 kph (40 mph). They feed mainly on grasses but also graze and browse on herbage, bushes and trees. The males form bachelor herds and females and young form separate herds, which may merge together during the dry season. A single calf is born after a gestation of 5–7 months and it is weaned at 4–6 months, and both sexes reach maturity at about 18 months, but males are not strong enough to hold territories until about 5 years old. In the wild, Impala may live to 12 years old; in captivity they have lived over 17 years. Impala are popular zoo exhibits and breed freely, often through several generations.

female

BLACKBUCK *Antilope cervicapra*

Originally Blackbuck were common and widespread in most of the open plains and scrub areas (the original 'jungles') of India, and Pakistan. The males are larger than the females and grow to a length of 1.2 m, plus a tail of 17 cm, stand up to 80 cm at the shoulder and weigh up to 40 kg. Only males carry horns, which are twisted in spirals up to 68.5 cm long. The males are also unusual among antelopes in their markedly different coloration from the females. At one time Blackbuck were probably the most abundant hoofed animal in India and occurred in herds

male

female

which numbered thousands of animals; now they are usually in herds of up to 50 and are comparatively rare. They were extensively hunted with cheetahs and later with guns. They are grazers, feeding on short grasses and sometimes cereal crops, resting during the hotter hours of the day. The young males form bachelor herds. The females and young are led by a mature male, which usually has the striking black coloration, although in the south of India they tend to be dark brown rather than black. During the breeding season the males are territorial, defending territories between 25 and 100 ha, and driving away any other males. The buck struts around, throws back its head and utters challenging grunts. After a gestation of about 6 months, a single calf (occasionally twins) is born and hidden in tall grass until strong enough to follow the rest of the herd. In captivity Blackbuck have lived for nearly 17 years.

A much rarer Indian antelope and one which is rarely seen in zoos is the Four-horned Antelope or Chowsingha, *Tetracerus quadricornis* which was once found widely in open wooded country throughout most of the Indian peninsula. As their name suggests, the most remarkable features of this antelope are its horns; although the females are hornless, the males have two pairs – the front pair are under half the length of the rear pair. The records are 7.6 cm for the front and 18.4 cm for the rear. The Four-horned Antelope is the only species of Bovidae to have 4 horns, although some domestic sheep have been bred with extra horns (such as Jacob's sheep).

SPRINGBOK *Antidorcas marsupialis*

The Springbok (or Springbuck) is the national emblem of the Republic of South Africa and was once one of the most numerous gazelles in Africa. It is now found in isolated populations in southern Africa. When European colonists first moved north from the Cape Colony, across the veldt, they found huge migrating herds of Springbok which numbered several million individuals and took several days to pass by. Even though their numbers are now greatly reduced, herds of up to 1500 occasionally occur. The last great trek of Springbok was in 1896 and spread over an area of 25 km wide and 220 km long, (15.5 miles × 137.5 miles). Like Lemming migrations in the Arctic, Springbok treks often ended at the sea where tens of thousands died on the coast. Springbok take their name from their habit of high, vertical, bouncing leaping (spronking) when agitated; these leaps may be repeated many times. When alarmed they can run at speeds of up to 90 kph (56 mph) and make single leaps of 15 m, in order to escape predators. They are preyed on by Lions, Leopards, Hyenas and Cheetah and the young are taken by smaller cats, jackals and eagles. The single young (rarely twins) is born after a gestation of up to 171 days. Springbok are regularly bred in many zoos, and have lived up to 19 years in captivity. They grow to a length of 1.4 m, plus a tail of up to 27 cm, stand up to 87 cm at the shoulder and weigh up to 36 kg; the males are slightly larger than females and both sexes carry horns. The males have horns of up to 48 cm, females up to 28 cm.

GERENUK *Litocranius walleri*

The Gerenuk is a long-legged, long-necked, gazelle with the strange habit of stretching up on its hind legs to browse on the higher parts of bushes. It is found in thorn and bush country in East Africa from Ethiopia and Somalia, south to Kenya and north-eastern Tanzania. It formerly had a wider distribution and within historical times occurred in Egypt. Gerenuks grow to a length of up to 1.6 m, a shoulder height of 1 m, and a weight of 50 kg; the males are larger than the females and carry fairly heavy horns about 35 cm long (up to 44 cm). They are well adapted to arid environments, and feed in a similar way to the Giraffe – plucking leaves with the tongue and long upper lip. In order to reach high branches they rest their forefeet against the tree or bush. Male Gerenuks hold territories, which they mark with dung and urine and secretions from glands above the eyes. The female gives birth to a single young after a gestation of 195–210 days. They are sexually mature at about 1 year old. In captivity they have lived over 13 years, but the maximum known in the wild is about 8 years. Gerenuks are rare in zoos, with only a few exhibited in the USA, and very few being captive bred.

The Dibatag *Ammodorcas clarkei* is even rarer in zoos. It resembles a rather slender-necked, small headed, lightly built Gerenuk, and shares the habit of clambering up to browse. It is restricted to the Horn of Africa.

DORCAS GAZELLE *Gazella dorcas*

The Dorcas Gazelle was once widespread over most
of North Africa from the Atlantic coast to Egypt and
the Red Sea coast and eastwards through the Levant
and Arabia to central India. Its present day range is
fragmented and many populations are rare or extinct.
A number of subspecies have been described, and
among those likely to be seen in zoos are the Arabian
Gazella dorcas saudiya and the Indian Chinkara *G.d.
bennetti*. The Dorcas Gazelle grows to 110 cm long,
plus a tail of up to 20 cm, and stands up to 65 cm at the
shoulder, and weighs up to 23 kg; both sexes carry
horns, up to a maximum of 40 cm in the male. Dorcas
Gazelles can survive in very arid areas, feeding in the
cooler parts of the day on plants including grasses,
leaves, melons, fruits and crops and getting moisture
from dew.

ADDRA GAZELLE *Gazella dama*

The Addra Gazelle (also known as the Dama) is found in arid, semi-desert areas of North Africa, where it is now extremely rare. It grows to a length of up to 1.6 m plus a tail of up to 35 cm, stands 1.2 m at the shoulder, and weighs up to 75 kg; both sexes carry horns, which can be up to 43 cm in the male. It can live for long periods without drinking water, existing entirely on dew and moisture in the plants it eats.

Other species of gazelle, closely related to the Addra and Dorcas, likely to be seen in zoos include the Mountain Gazelle or Idmi *Gazella gazella*, from the Middle East, and the Persian or Goitred Gazelle *G. subguttorosa*, from Arabia east to Pakistan and Mongolia. Both are being bred in zoos. *NB*: There has often been considerable confusion with the Latin names of gazelles.

GRANT'S GAZELLE *Gazella granti*

Grant's Gazelle is found in East Africa from southern Ethiopia and Somalia south to central Tanzania and west to Lake Victoria and Lake Rudolf. It is a relatively large gazelle growing to a length of 1.5 m, plus a tail of up to 35 cm, standing up to 95 cm at the shoulder and weighing up to 80 kg; males are larger than females but both sexes carry horns which, in the male, grow to 80 cm. It is closely related to Soemmerring's Gazelle *G. soemmerringi*, from Ethiopia, Somalia and the Sudan. Both species have a gestation of about 199 days, after which a single young is born. The young remain hidden for several days after birth, being visited by the mother for suckling. In captivity Grant's Gazelles have lived nearly 9 years, Soemmering's up to 14 years.

THOMSON'S GAZELLE *Gazella thomsoni*

Thomson's Gazelle is a familiar sight in National Parks and Game Reserves in East Africa. It is found from the southern Sudan, through Kenya to northern Tanzania. It grows to a length of up to 1.1 m, plus a tail of up to 27 cm, stands 65 cm at the shoulder and weighs up to 30 kg. Both sexes carry horns, the male's grow up to 43 cm long, but the female's are less than 15 cm. 'Tommies' as they are popularly known, live in the open plains, feeding mainly on grasses. A single young is born at almost any time of the year after a gestation of up to 188 days, and reaches maturity at 1–1½ years; in captivity they have lived for over 10 years. The Red-fronted Gazelle *Gazella rufifrons* of the sub-Saharan region, is closely related to Thomson's, but only rarely exhibited in zoos.

SAIGA *Saiga tatarica*

The recent history of the Saiga is one of the major conservation successes. The Saiga is an antelope of the grassy steppes and plains, often very arid, of Central Asia. It grows to a length of up to 1.4 m, plus a tail of 13 cm, stands up to 80 cm and weighs up to 69 kg; the males carry horns which may grow up to 25 cm. It has a rather shaggy coat to protect it from the bitterly cold winds and winter temperatures, but its most characteristic feature is its enlarged proboscis-like nose. Its exact function is not known, but it may be for warming the air it breathes and since it is lined with hair it may be for filtering dust. The Saiga has been exterminated from much of its original range by the beginning of the 20th century; as long ago as the thirteenth century it had disappeared from the Crimean steppes, but a few survived in the Ukraine until the eighteenth century. However, even these were finally exterminated, until by the beginning of the twentieth century only about 1,000 were left, and these were still being killed for their horns which were sold in the Far East as medicines. Immediately after the Bolshevik revolution, Saiga were protected, and by 1958 the population had grown to about 2 million, and once again a limited harvest is allowed. They range over an area of 2,500,000 sq km, wintering to the west of the Caspian. They form large herds during their migrations, but normally live in groups of about 30–40. A single calf or twins is born after a gestation of up to 152 days, and they are active soon after birth, and start grazing at around 1 week. The females are mature within a year and they are known to live up to 12 years in the wild. Outside the USSR they are comparatively rare in zoos.

female

male

SEROWS

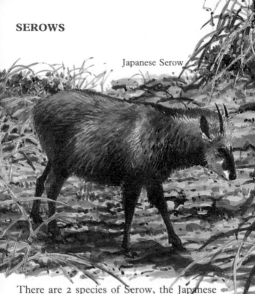

Japanese Serow

There are 2 species of Serow, the Japanese Serow *Capricornis crispus*, occurring on the islands of Honshu, Shikoku, and Kynshu in Japan and on Taiwan, and the Mainland Serow *C. sumatrensis*, which is found from central China and the Himalayas south through Thailand, Burma and Malaya to Sumatra. The Japanese Serow, the species most likely to be seen in zoos, grows to about

1.6 m long, plus a bushy tail of up to 16 cm, stands up to 90 cm at the shoulder and weighs up to about 100 kg. Both sexes carry horns which are rather small, growing to a maximum of 25 cm. Despite its wide range, the slightly larger Mainland Serow is very rare in captivity. Serows are also known as Goat-antelopes, together with the Gorals *Nemorhaedus* of the Himalayas, Tibet and Burma, and they are in some ways like a rather heavily built, large-headed Chamois. They are extremely sure-footed, living in thickly wooded ravines, and on mountainsides, where they often have well defined paths along cliffs and ledges. They generally live alone, but occasionally small groups of up to 4 or 5 may be seen feeding together in the early morning or late evening. They feed on grasses, leaves and shoots. When they are alarmed, Serow make off with a snort; they also call to one another with a whistling scream. The rut begins in late summer and a single young is born after a gestation of about 7 months. In captivity Serows have lived for over 10 years. The population on Taiwan has been described as a separate subspecies, *C. crispus swinhoe* and is smaller than all other serows. The Sumatran subspecies of the Mainland Serow *C. sumatrensis sumatrensis* has become very reduced in numbers; although its flesh is not particularly sought after for human food, various parts of the animals, including the horns and some internal organs, are believed to have medicinal properties in the Far East. In addition much of the serow's habitat has been destroyed or is threatened.

MOUNTAIN GOAT *Oreamnos americanus*

The Mountain Goat once ranged across the mountainous regions of North America from southeastern Alaska through Canada to Oregon and Montana. It is not a true goat, but related to the Chamois. From the 1920s onwards they have been reintroduced into areas from which they had been exterminated and also introduced into new areas, such as Oregon, Nevada, Utah, Colorado, Wyoming, and South Dakota. Mountain Goats are up to 2 m long, plus a short tail of up to 20 cm, and can weigh up to 113 kg, but average 85 kg. The males are up to $\frac{1}{3}$ larger than females, and carry larger horns than the females; an average horn length is 23 cm, but they can be up to 30 cm. They inhabit very rugged inaccessible parts of the mountains, feeding on grasses, sedges and forbs, often perched on ledges or in the alpine meadows. They are preyed on by Pumas, eagles, Brown Bears, Wolves and Coyotes, particularly when young. The rutting season is in late autumn; when courting a female (nannie) the male (billy) approaches her and gives her a quick kick in the side! The males rarely actually fight, but when they do, their short horns can inflict serious wounds. The young – usually a single kid, but twins are not rare, and triplets occur occasionally – are born after a gestation of about 178 days, in late spring or early summer. The kids follow their mother very closely and are weaned by late summer, but follow the mother until the following spring. Both sexes mature at about $2\frac{1}{2}$ years; in the wild they have been known to live for up to 18 years.

CHAMOIS *Rupicapra rupicapra*

summer pelage

The Chamois, whose soft Chamois, or 'shammy', leather is used for cleaning glass and other highly polished surfaces, is native to the mountains of southern Europe, Asia Minor and the Caucasus. Most populations are isolated from each other. Chamois grow to a length of up to 1.3 m plus a tail of up to 40 cm, stand up to 80 cm at the shoulder and weigh up to 50 kg. Both sexes carry slender horns, up to 20 cm long. Females and young (lambs) normally live in small herds, of up to 30 animals, and are joined by adult males in winter. The lambs (usually one, but twins and triplets occur) are born after a gestation of up to 210 days. They follow their mother within an hour or so of birth and within a few days are agile leapers; if their mother is killed the young attach themselves to other females. They can live for up to 22 years. In the past over-hunting has caused the local extermination of the Chamois, particularly in the European parts of its range. The flesh is highly prized and despite their small size, their horns are sought-after trophies; the thick winter fur is used to make tufts known as 'gamsbart' which adorn Tyrolean hats. Chamois have been introduced into New Zealand; 10 were released between 1907 and 1913, and they are now numerous at altitudes of up to 3223 m (10,475 ft). The Appenine subspecies of Chamois *R. rupicapra ornata* is found only in the Abruzzo National Park in Italy where less than 500 survive.

Chamois in winter pelage and Alpine Chough

MUSK OX *Ovibos moschatus*

Within historical times the Musk Ox occurred from Alaska to Greenland, and until about 2000 years ago was found in the Arctic regions of the Old World. They were exterminated in Alaska, and in the 1930s reduced to about 500 on the Canadian mainland but conservation measures have allowed the population to increase to about 25,000 and they have been introduced into Alaska, USSR, Norway and elsewhere. They grow up to 2.3 m long, stand up to 1.5 m at the shoulder and weigh up to 400 kg (in captivity up to 650 kg). Musk Ox live exclusively in Arctic tundra, in herds of 15–20 animals, occasionally up to 100. When approached by an intruder the herd forms a defensive circle or line, with the calves behind. Although this defence is effective against Wolves (their main natural predator) it allowed human hunters to slaughter them with ease. Around the turn of the century they were important as fur animals and some 15,000 skins were traded by the Hudson's Bay Company from 1862 until 1917 when they were given complete protection; in addition, large numbers were killed by the native Eskimos. Musk Oxen feed on low tundra vegetation, particularly grasses, dwarf willow, sedges, moss and lichen.

During the rut, the dominant male drives all other mature males from the herd. The fighting during the rut includes head-on charges at speeds of up to 40 kph. Mating takes place in spring–early summer, and the single young (occasionally twins) is born after a gestation of 8–9 months. The calf is active from birth and begins to eat vegetation at about 1 week. In the wild they have lived up to 23 years. Musk Oxen do not adapt to warm climates well, and are consequently rather unusual in zoos.

Musk Oxen in defensive line

HIMALAYAN TAHR *Hemitragus jemlahicus*

The Himalayan Tahr occurs throughout the Himalayas, where it lives among inaccessible and precipitous cliffs at altitudes above 3000 m, but not above the tree line. They live in dense forest, hiding in the shade of oak and other trees and bushes, rarely coming into the open once the sun is high in the sky. Small numbers (5 in 1904 and 8 in 1909) were taken from the Duke of Bedford's herd in Woburn, England and released in the southern Alps of New Zealand. They throve, lacking any predators or natural competitors, now number between 20,000 and 30,000 and are now extensively hunted. Tahr have also been introduced on the Table Mountain in South Africa. Himalayan Tahr grow to a shoulder height of up to 100 cm, and a weight of 90 kg. Both sexes carry horns, but the females rarely exceed 25 cm; the record male horns are nearly 42 cm. Tahr live in herds, and the males rut in winter. During the rut, the males fight fiercely, and since their habitat is so precipitous a fight can often end in one of the contestors plunging to his death. The single young (occasionally twins) is born in late spring or early summer after a gestation of up to 242 days (but usually less). The Himalayan Tahr is often exhibited in zoos, where they breed freely and have lived for over 21 years.

There are 2 other closely related species of Tahr: the Nilgiri Tahr *H. hylocrius* found in southern India and the Arabian Tahr *H. jayakari*, confined to Oman. Poaching and habitat destruction have reduced the Nilgiri Tahr to a population of about 2230 animals. The Arabian Tahr exists in even smaller numbers, due to poaching and competition with goats, but in recent years has been given considerable protection by the government of Oman. There are small numbers of Nilgiri Tahr in a few American zoos.

MARKHOR *Capra falconeri*

The Markhor is found in the western Himalayas, from Kashmir, and the Hindu Kush, west to Turkmenia, living at high altitudes, but rarely going above the snowline. In winter they move down to lower levels. But there is considerable variation in their habitat throughout their range, and also considerable variation in their magnificent spiral horns. Several subspecies have been described, based mainly on the shape of the horns. They grow to a shoulder height of about 1 m and the horns grow to over 1 m, with a record set from Pir Panjal measuring over 1.65 m. Males stand up to 1 m at the shoulder; females are only about half the size of a well grown male. Old males gradually become almost white; females are usually dark fawn and occasionally have a short beard, but never the flowing beard of the male. Like other goats, Markhor live in herds but, unlike most other species, in Pakistan some males have been observed to remain with the females throughout the year. The rut takes place from October–December, and 1 or 2 kids are born in late spring or early summer. Some biologists believe that Markhor may be one of the ancestors of domesticated goats, and they will hybridise with most other species of sheep.

Markhor are one of the rarest wild goats, and the Kabul or Straight-horned Makrhor *C. falconeri megaceros* is one of the rarest of all.

The 2 species of Blue sheep or Bharal *Pseudois* spp. from Central Asia, are only rarely seen in zoos; in appearance they are somewhat intermediate between sheep and goats.

IBEX *Capra ibex*

The Ibex or Steinbok is found in the Alps in Europe, in the Himalayas, and in the mountains of central Asia, Arabia and north Africa. They are very agile and usually live among rocky mountain crags. At one time the European population was reduced to a single population in the Gran Paradiso National Park, but has now been re-established in many parts of the Alps. The Ibex is very closely related to the Spanish Ibex *C. pyrenaica*, which is found in several mountain areas in the Iberian peninsula; the ends of its horns twist outwards. The Ethiopian population, the Walia *C. ibex walia*, is sometimes regarded as a separate species.

The Ibex lives mostly above the treeline in Europe. The males rut in winter and the clashing of their horns can often be heard for several kilometres. The single kid (occasionally twins) is born in early summer after a gestation of up to 180 days. Ibex are often hunted, and many populations are rare or extinct; the Walia is one of the rarest with less than 300, and the Pyranean population of the Spanish Ibex may number less than 20. Several subspecies of Ibex are exhibited in zoos, where they often breed freely; these include the Alpine Ibex *C. ibex ibex*, Siberian Ibex *C.i. sibirica*, and Nubian Ibex *C.i. nubiana*. Captive Ibex have lived for over 22 years. The closely related East Caucasian Tur *C. cylindricornis* and West Caucasian Tur *C. caucasica* are also kept in a few zoos.

The Wild Goat *C. aegagrus* which occurs on Crete and some other Greek Islands, and in parts of Asia Minor, and the Middle East and Pakistan, is also similar to the Ibex. It is not known with any certainty which goats were the source of domestic goats and they may interbreed at times, but the most important ancestor is the Wild Goat.

BARBARY SHEEP *Ammotragus lervia*

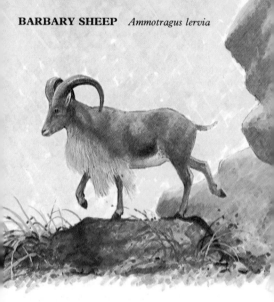

The Barbary Sheep or Aoudad has long been a popular exhibit in zoos, but is now rare in the wild. It was once found across the Saharan region from the southern slopes of the Atlas Mountains east to Egypt and the Sudan; it possibly also occurred in Sinai and the Levant. It is intermediate between sheep and goats, and shares characteristics with both. Barbary

Sheep grow to a length of up to 1.6 m plus a tail of 25 cm, stand 1.1 m at the shoulder and weigh up to 145 kg; the males are considerably larger than females, and have horns of up to 88 cm, twice the size of the females. They feed mostly in the morning or early evening, resting in the shade during the hotter parts of the day; they feed on grasses and leaves of bushes, which they often reach by standing on their hind legs. They are preyed on by Leopard and Caracal, and formerly by Lions but the latter are now extinct within the range of Barbary Sheep. Because of the lack of cover within the habitat, the Barbary Sheep normally avoid detection by freezing. They also sand-bath which may help dust their hair to the same colour as their habitat. Lambs are mostly born in March–May, after a gestation of up to 161 days, but can be born at any time of the year; females are known to have had 2 births in a year, normally single young, but twins are common and triplets are sometimes born. Soon after birth the young are following the mother over the most precipitous terrain. In captivity Barbary Sheep have lived 24 years. Although they have disappeared from many of their former strongholds in the Sahara, through overhunting, they thrive in zoos and parks where several hundred are bred each year, and they have been self-sustaining for several decades. They have also been introduced into the southern states of the USA for sport hunting, are thriving in California, New Mexico and Texas and sufficiently abundant to be possibly competing with the native Big-horn Sheep (p. 398).

AMERICAN MOUNTAIN SHEEP

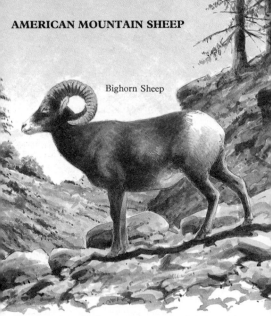

Bighorn Sheep

The American Bighorn, *Ovis canadensis* is found in mountains of North America from southwest Canada to northern Mexico. Dall's Sheep *O. dalli*, has a more northerly distribution ranging from the northern Canadian Rockies, to Alaska. Both species are under threat from competition with other native ungulates such as deer, domestic livestock and from introduced species (see Barbary Sheep p. 396). In the past many of the rangelands of wild sheep were periodically burned but in the last half century these fires have been largely controlled, and this has led to forest encroachment. Both species are primarily grazers, eating mostly grasses, but also willows, sedges and flowering plants. The Bighorn grows to a length of up to 1.6 m, plus a tail of 11 cm, stands 42 cm at the shoulder and weighs up to 150 kg. The males are larger than the females and although both sexes carry horns, the males are much larger. The horns of a mature male Bighorn are, proportionally, the largest of all ruminants (up to 12% of the rams weight), growing to nearly 80 cm. Dall's Sheep is slightly smaller and more lightly built than the Bighorn. During the rut the rams clash head-on with a crash audible nearly 2 kms away. After a gestation of 180 days a single lamb (occasionally twins) is born with a soft woolly, fawn-coloured coat. For their first week they remain hidden then they follow the mother. The breeding of Dall's Sheep is similar to Bighorn.

Dall Sheep

MOUFLON *Ovis orientalis*

The Mouflon, or Wild Sheep, is the ancestor of all the domestic varieties of sheep. They are found on Cyprus, Corsica and Sardinia (but were probably introduced by man in ancient times when still little different from the wild sheep of Asia Minor), Asia Minor and east to Iran. It has been extensively introduced into central and southern Europe as a game animal. Several populations of the Mouflon are rare or endangered, but Mouflon are often seen in zoos, where they breed freely. Domestic sheep (including primitive breeds such as the Soay sheep in the Outer Hebrides) are distinguished from wild species, such as Mouflon, by having a coat made up mostly of wool, without the hair that covers the wool in wild sheep.

Mouflon grow to about 1.2 m long, stand up to 75 cm at the shoulder and weigh about 32 kg (males). The males carry large curved horns. Females and their lambs live in flocks all the year round; the males form separate flocks and single males join the female flock during the autumn rut. The lambs which may be single or twins, are born after a gestation of up to 180 days. Mouflon are mainly grazers, feeding primarily on grasses. They are mainly nocturnal, hiding in dense cover during daylight hours.

There are over 800 different breeds of domestic sheep, numbering perhaps 800-million individual sheep. Sheep are bred for 3 main purposes; wool, meat and milk, although milking sheep are becoming rare, as are many of the more specialised breeds. Fortunately, some of the rarer breeds are now being revived and some zoos keep small flocks, often in the childrens' section.

RED SHEEP OR URIAL *Ovis vignei*

The Urial or Shapu is found from Iran and
Turkestan eastwards to Afghanistan, Pakistan,
Kashmir and north-west India and Tibet, and south
to Oman. It is closely related to the Mouflon and in
northern Iran they interbreed in some places where
their ranges overlap. The Urial stands about 90 cm at
the shoulder and weighs up to 60 kg. Both sexes carry
horns but the females are small, those of the male are
larger and rather variable in shape, growing to over
100 cm long; the largest come from the Punjab, where
they are strongly wrinkled and usually curved in a

circular sweep. In Afghanistan the horns often turn outwards in an open spiral. The habitat varies with location, but generally Urial live at high altitudes, on open grassy mountain slopes, or rocky scrub-covered hills, generally in inaccessible areas. They undergo seasonal movements, retreating from the higher altitudes in winter. Like other sheep and goats they are gregarious and live in flocks. The older rams live in bachelor flocks outside the rutting season which is in autumn. During the rut the rams gather in small groups of 3 or 4 ewes. Single or twin lambs are born in late spring or early summer. The Urial has already become extinct in many places and in most parts of its range is declining. Urials are exhibited in a few zoos, where they breed freely.

The Argali *Ovis ammon* is a closely related wild sheep found from southern Siberia and central Asia, south to the Himalayas and northern China. It is the largest of the sheep standing up to 120 cm at the shoulder. A number of distinct subspecies have been described, the most impressive of which is known as Marco Polo's Sheep *O. ammon polii*, which has massive curved horns, growing to 1.69 m long. Most populations of Argali have declined and in the USSR most are considered rare or endangered. Argali are rarely seen in zoos.

PANGOLINS

Cape Pangolin

Pangolins are confined to the Old World, with 3 species found in southern Asia and 4 in Africa. The largest species, the Giant Ground Pangolin *Manis gigantea* is found in Africa in savannah country from Senegal and Uganda south to Angola. It grows to a total length of 1.75 m and weighs up to 35 kg. The Cape or Temminck's Ground Pangolin *M. temmincki* is also found in open bush country, from the Sudan south through East Africa to Botswana, Namibia and South Africa (except the southern Cape!)

There are two species of tree pangolin in Africa, the Long-tailed or Black-bellied *Manis tetradactyla* and the White-bellied *M. tricuspis*. Both species are found in rainforests from Senegal west to north-east Zaire and Uganda and south to Angola. The Black-bellied Pangolin grows to a length of 40 cm plus a tail of up to 80 cm and weighs up to 3.25 kg; the White-bellied Pangolin is slightly smaller, with a proportionally shorter tail. Both species are nocturnal, hiding in tree holes by day and are excellent climbers. On the underside of the tail they have a naked area, which is used as a prehensile grip when they are climbing. They feed on ants and termites, which they extract from under bark, in fungi etc. with their long extendable tongue. The White-bellied Pangolin gives birth to a single young which stays in the nest hole for the first week and is then carried on the mother's tail. They start to eat insects at about 2 weeks and are independent at about 4–5 months and are driven away at about 7–8 months. The Black-bellied Pangolin's reproduction is similar. In captivity they have lived 3 years, but the Indian Pangolin *M. crassicaudata* has lived over 13 years. The Asian Pangolins are extensively hunted because of the alleged medicinal value of their scales, which are used in the Far East to treat skin diseases. Although pangolins are occasionally exhibited in zoos they do not appear to thrive and are rarely bred.

White-bellied Pangolin

SQUIRRELS (1)

Giant Forest Squirrel

There are 2 species of Giant Forest Squirrels, the Slender-tailed Giant Forest Squirrel *Protoxerus aubinni* found in West Africa from Liberia to Ghana; and the Oil-palm Squirrel *P. stangeri* which ranges from Sierra Leone to Kenya and Angola. They grow to a length of up to 33 cm, plus a tail of up to 38 cm, and weigh up to 2¾ kg. They live mostly in the upper branches of the forest trees, feeding on oil palm fruits, nuts, fruit and other vegetable matter, occasionally birds and other animals, and known as 'ivory eaters' from their habit of gnawing bones and ivory. They are occasionally seen in zoos as are a number of other species, in particular the Oriental Giant Squirrels *Ratufa* spp. from southern Asia, which are 2 or 3 times the size of the African species.

The American Grey Squirrel *Sciurus carolinensis* is widespread in south-eastern Canada and eastern USA and have been introduced in several places in the western states, and into Britain. They grow to a length of up to 30 cm, plus a tail of up to 25 cm, and weigh up to ¾ kg. The Grey Squirrel was bred in zoos and private collections in Britain at the end of the last century. Some released into Regent's Park from London Zoo and elsewhere flourished and rapidly spread. It is now found over most of England and Wales, as well as parts of Scotland and Wales, and in many areas appears to have displaced the native Red Squirrel *Sciurus vulgaris*, (p. 407–8). Although exhibited occasionally, few zoos have regularly breeding colonies. Grey Squirrels normally have 2 litters a year of about 3 young; the young are blind and helpless and do not emerge from the nest (drey) until about 2 months old. In the USA this is an important game animal, with about 40-million killed every year.

Grey Squirrel

SQUIRRELS (2)

Indian Palm
Squirrel

Red Squirrel

The Indian or Three-striped Palm Squirrel *Funambulus palmarum* is one of the 5 species of Palm or Striped Squirrels found in the Indian subcontinent and Ceylon. It is found in central and southern India and Sri Lanka in forests where its repetitive, shrill, birdlike call can be heard. They feed on fruits, nuts, bark and other vegetable matter, and occasionally insects, birds' eggs; they also drink nectar, and are probably important in pollinating some trees such as silk cotton trees (kapok). The females build round nests in a tree where they give birth to litters of 1–5, up to 3 times a year, after a gestation of up to 45 days.

The Red Squirrel *Sciurus vulgaris* is widespread across the Old World from Ireland to Hokkaido in the Far East. It is found in coniferous and mixed forests. In the British Isles its populations have fluctuated widely; it became extinct in Ireland, but was subsequently reintroduced, and in England it is now all but extinct and has been replaced by the Grey Squirrel (p. 407). It grows to a length of up to 25 cm, plus a tail of up to 20 cm. In Britain its tail and ear tufts gradually bleach until, just before they moult in early summer, they are nearly white. In continental Europe and other parts of their range dark, almost black, animals are often common.

In North America 2 species of Red Squirrel occur: the Eastern or American Red Squirrel *Tamiasciurus hudsonicus* and Douglas' Squirrel *T. douglasi*. Although both the Old and New World red squirrels are sometimes seen in zoos, they do not appear to be bred on a regular basis.

PRAIRIE DOGS AND MARMOTS

Alpine Marmot

Woodchuck

Prairie Dog

There are 11 species of marmots, found in the more temperate parts of the northern hemisphere. One of the best known species in the Old World is the Alpine Marmot *Marmota marmota* which is found above the treeline in the Alps and the Carpathians and has been introduced into the Pyrenees. It grows to a length of 70 cm, plus a tail of 15 cm, and weighs up to 8 kg. It lives in colonies and emerges from the burrows as the sun strikes the mountain side to sunbathe before feeding. During the winter months it hibernates.

The Woodchuck *M. monax*, is found in the north-eastern states of the USA, much of Canada and southeastern Alaska. It is slightly smaller than the Alpine Marmot, and lives in open wooded habitats. There are several other closely related species in North America including the rare Vancouver Island Marmot *M. vancouverensis*, and the Olympic Marmot *M. olympus*, confined to the Alpine zone of the Olympic mountains in Washington.

Prairie dogs are ground-dwelling squirrels super-ficially similar to the Marmots. The most widespread is the Black-tailed Prairie Dog *Cynomys ludovicianus*, which grows to a length of 31 cm, plus a tail of 9.5 cm and weighs up to 1.3 kg. It lives in colonies, known as 'towns', and because of its burrowing activities has been exterminated over much of its range. Alpine Marmots and Woodchucks are both kept in zoos in small numbers where they occasionally breed.

The Prairie Dog is often seen in zoos, several of which have thriving colonies, such as the one at Whipsnade.

EUROPEAN SOUSLIKS

European Suslik

Spotted Suslik

The 2 species of sousliks or ground squirrels found in Europe are closely related to another 30 species found in northern Asia and North America. The European Souslik *Spermophilus citellus* is found in open steppe country from south-eastern Germany and southern Poland, southwards to Yugoslavia, Bulgaria and Greece. The Spotted Souslik *S. souslicus* occurs in open steppe country from Romania and Poland eastwards to the River Volga in the USSR. The European Souslik grows to 22 cm plus a tail of 7.5 cm and weighs up to 340 gms; the Spotted Souslik is a similar size, but has a shorter tail. They are both colonial and active by day. They make a variety of noises, including whistles and growls, and often one or more stand sentinel, keeping watch for predators. They excavate burrows, which are often very extensive. As soon as they emerge from hibernation they start breeding, producing a single litter of 6–8 young after a gestation of up to 1 month. In the past sousliks caused extensive damage to crops, but in recent years have undergone considerable declines in most parts of Europe due to changes in agriculture. In North America sousliks are usually known as ground squirrels. Most are rather similar in habits to the European species, but some are rather chipmunk-like. Despite their abundance in the wild, Souslik are not often exhibited in zoos, and no zoo appears to have a regular breeding colony.

CHIPMUNKS

Eastern Chipmunk

There are about 23 species of chipmunk, all of which are found in North America, except for the Siberian Chipmunk *Tamias sibiricus*. The most widespread and common species in eastern USA and Canada is the Eastern Chipmunk *T. striatus*, which is slightly larger than most other chipmunks, growing to a length of up to 18 cm, plus a tail of up to 11 cm and weighing up to 142 gms. They live in deciduous forests and more open areas with bushes and ground cover, living in burrows, in tunnels under logs or among rock crevices. In addition to their nesting burrows they also have chambers for storing foods such as nuts, acorns and corn. They also eat fungi, fruits and berries, and will occasionally eat insects, birds' eggs and small mammals. They have cheek pouches on either side of the head, each of which can be extended to almost the size of the head. The females often produce two litters a year of 1–9 young, after a gestation of about 31 days. The young leave the nest at about 6 weeks, disperse and are independent at 8 weeks, and breed the following year. In the wild Eastern Chipmunks have lived for 2–3 years, in captivity for up to 8 years. Although they are often common they are rarely serious pests, and are often popular garden visitors in North America, visiting bird feeders. During the winter months they often hibernate. They are preyed on by a wide variety of birds of prey as well as Raccoons, Foxes, Weasels and, in suburban areas, domestic cats. Although popular as pets and often exhibited in zoos, self-sustaining captive populations do not appear to exist.

Goshawk with Siberian Chipmunk

FLYING SQUIRREL

Siberian Flying Squirrel

There are a large number of flying squirrels, though, in fact, they are not capable of true flight: squirrels can merely glide. Non-flying squirrels have often been observed to spread-eagle their limbs and arch their tail when falling from a tree to the ground – a fall of 180 m has been recorded, from which the squirrel was unhurt. The flying squirrels have developed the ability to glide using a membrane which stretches between the fore and hind limbs, and in some species between the hind limbs and the tail. Most of the 35 flying squirrels are found in Asia, and in particular the forests of Indo-China and South-east Asia. The largest species are the Giant Flying Squirrels *Petaurista* spp which grow to over 50 cm long plus a tail of up to 60 cm, and weigh up to 2.5 kg. They have been observed to make glides of up to 450 m, and have been seen to use air currents in deep valleys. Outside eastern southern Asia only 4 species are found: 2 in the Old World: the Siberian Flying Squirrel *Pteromys volans*, and a closely related species from Japan, and 2 from the New World: the Northern Flying Squirrel *Glaucomys sabrinus* and the Southern Flying Squirrel *Glaucomys volans*. The Siberian Flying Squirrel is sometimes exhibited in zoos, but they are strictly nocturnal and so only exhibited in zoos with 'reverse lighting'. Siberian Flying Squirrels are found right across the northern mature forests of the Old World from Finland to Siberia, Korea and Hokkaido. They are extremely agile, and can manoeuvre in flight. Outside the breeding season they sometimes gather in small groups in a single tree, but these colonies are of one sex. They grow to about 17 cm, plus a tail of up to 13 cm. The Southern Flying Squirrel is slightly larger and the Northern even larger still, growing to about 30 cm plus a tail of 14.5 cm. The American species are very similar in appearance to the Siberian. They have been observed to glide 50 m from a starting height of 15 m.

SMALL RODENTS

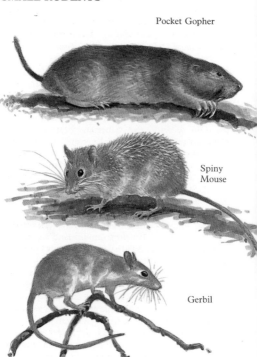

Pocket Gopher

Spiny
Mouse

Gerbil

It is usually only the larger or more scientific zoos which exhibit some of the smaller, less spectacular animals. Although there are over 1600 species of rodents only a tiny handful of them are ever seen in zoos. The Pocket Gopher family (*Geomyidae*) comprises some 37 species found in North and Central America. They are burrowing animals, and their lips can be closed behind their front teeth so that they can use them to dig without getting mouthfuls of soil. Their name derives from the fur-lined pouches on the sides of the head used for carrying food.

The 5 species of Spiny mice *Acomys* spp, occur in Africa, and the Middle East. The most familiar is the Cairo Spiny Mouse *A. cahirinus* which is found across north Africa, through the Middle East to Pakistan, and also on the island of Crete. They are very adaptable and live on dry seeds and grasses, and have also been reported eating the dried flesh of the mummies in Egyptian tombs.

There are over 70 species of gerbils and jirds, which are found in the steppes and arid regions of Africa, and central and western Asia. Most species are relatively easy to keep in captivity and breed freely, and a large number have been kept in laboratories, and a few are kept in larger zoos. The most frequently seen is the Mongolian, or Clawed Jird *Meriones unguiculatus*, which is the species most frequently sold in pet shops under the name 'Gerbil'. There is a serious risk, both in North America and parts of Europe, that if pets were to escape they could become serious pests.

BEAVERS

Canadian Beaver

There are 2 species of beaver: the American Beaver *Castor canadensis* which was once widespread over North America as far as northern Mexico, and the Eurasian Beaver, *C. fiber*, which was once found over most of Europe, except the southern peninsulas, and east through the USSR to the Altai. They are among the world's largest rodents growing to

80 cm plus a tail of up to 45 cm and weighing up to 25 kg, occasionally 40 kg. The preferred habitat is well-wooded slow flowing rivers and marshes with bushes and undergrowth. They build dams, dig canals and tunnels and construct lodges, depending on the habitat, in order to regulate the water level and transport logs. Although they normally fell fairly small trees, they have been recorded to fell trees up to 1 m in diameter. Beavers usually pair for life and mate in January or February. The young are born April–June. There are 2–4 young in a litter, which become independent when they are nearly 2 years old. In the wild they are believed to have lived for at least 21 years. Beavers have been extensively hunted for their fur, which was 'felted' for high quality hats, and for the *castoreum* from the scent glands. In early Christian Europe they could also be eaten during fasts as fish – on account of their scaly tail. Beavers have been exterminated from most of Europe, including Britain, but some recent introduction programmes have been successful. The American Beaver was one of the mainstays of the economy during the early colonial explorations of New England and Canada; it was also hunted to extinction in many areas. They are still of considerable importance to the fur trade and unlike many other fur-bearing species, they are not normally farmed or ranched. In recent years they have been reintroduced into many parts of the United States. Beavers are exhibited in some zoos, and a few are now breeding them regularly.

SPRING HARE *Pedetes capensis*

The Spring Hare or Springhaas (the Afrikaans name) is not a true hare but a rabbit-sized, kangaroo-like rodent. It grows to a length of up to 43 cm, and weighs up to 4 kg. Spring Hares are found in open plains, lightly wooded savannahs and bush country, usually in arid areas, with sandy soils. They dig burrows and may spend the daytime in different burrows on successive days; the burrows can be up to 40 m or more long. They are normally nocturnal, emerging around dusk, and staying in their burrow during heavy rains. When sleeping they tuck their heads down between their hind legs and curl the tail around the head and body. They normally live singly or in small family groups, but often close to other Spring Hares, so that groups of 30 or more can sometimes be encountered in feeding areas. They feed mainly on roots and grasses and other plants, and occasionally insects such as locusts. After a gestation of up to 82 days single young (twins very rarely) are born. Although they can run when about 2 days old, they remain in the burrow until well grown. They are weaned at 6–7 weeks and most females have several litters a year. In captivity Spring Hares will live in groups without fighting; although they are bred in a few zoos there do not appear to be any really thriving populations.

HAMSTERS

Common Hamster

The 15 species of hamsters are found in the grasslands and open steppes of central and eastern Europe and Asia. The best known is undoubtedly the Golden Hamster *Mesocricetus auratus*. Although the best known species, it has a very restricted range, and is only known from Aleppo in northern Syria. In 1930 a female was captured, together with her litter: 1 male and 2 females eventually survived and started a breeding colony. In 1931 some were sent to Britain and in 1938 they were first taken to the USA. They are now bred by the hundreds of thousands, both as pets and laboratory animals, and a wide range of colour varieties, long-haired and other mutations have been developed. Golden Hamsters are prolific, breeding when they are about 7 or 8 weeks old, and having litters of 2–16 (average 9) after a gestation of 16 days. When new-born young are disturbed the mother will often put them in her cheek pouches and remove them to a safer site.

Brandt's Golden Hamster *M. brandti* is closely related to the Golden Hamster but is found over a much wider area, from the Levant, east to northern Iraq and Iran. In recent decades laboratory colonies have been started successfully. The two species of dwarf hamsters *Phodopus sungorus* and *P. roborovskii* are both being kept in a number of zoos and being bred freely. The rat-like hamsters *Cricetulus* spp., which include the Grey Hamster *C. migratorius* of south-eastern Europe, are occasionally exhibited as is the Common Hamster *Cricetus cricetus* from central Europe and Asia. In Europe hamsters were once serious agricultural pests, but with the changes in farming practices in most parts of Europe they have declined or even become extinct.

Golden Hamster

RATS

Black Rat

There are around 80 species of true rats *Rattus* in the world, but possibly more await discovery. They include some highly adaptable species, such as the Black or Ship Rat *R. rattus* which has spread to most parts of the world associated with humans; the Brown or Norway Rat *R. norvegicus* which is also a human associate and found almost worldwide; and the Polynesian Rat *R. exulans* from Burma and Indo-China which humans have spread all over the Pacific. These and some other rats cause enormous damage to agricultural produce and other property and are responsible for the spread of epidemic diseases such as Bubonic plagues. The Brown Rat is also the ancestor of the domesticated laboratory rats, and the various 'fancy' pet rats. There are many species of rat confined to small areas, particularly in the Far East, and some of these may become rare as forests are destroyed.

Some of the rats and mice found in south-east Asia are only known from a few museum skins and have not been studied alive. Among these are 2 species of *Phyloeomys* from the Philippines. The Luzon Cloud Rat *P. pallidus* is confined to the northern parts of the island, where there is a number of other mammals, found nowhere else in the world, which are likely to disappear as their forest habitat disappears. The Slender-tailed Rat *P. cumingi* is found on southern Luzon and also on the islands of Mindora and Marinduque. Cloud rats are among the largest of the true rats and mice growing to a length of up to 48 cm plus a tail of up to 35 cm and weighing up to 2 kg. They thrive in captivity, and have given birth to a single young which the mother carries attached to her nipple; they have lived over 13 years in captivity. Little is known of their biology and even less about their habits and status in the wild.

A few zoos exhibit the Multi-mammate Rat *Praomys natalensis*, one of the African soft-furred rats, so called because they may have as many as 24 nipples. In many parts of Africa it is the common rat, associated with human settlements and agriculture. They have litters of up to 22 young and can breed when under 4 months old, so their populations can grow very rapidly. However, in many areas it is being pushed out by Black Rats.

Bushy-tailed Cloud Rat
Crateromys schadenbergi from Luzon in the Phillipines

DORMICE

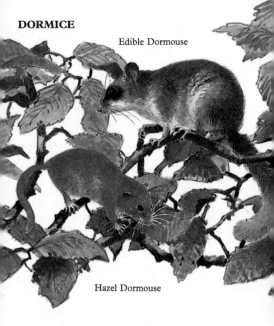

Edible Dormouse

Hazel Dormouse

This family of some 14 species is confined to the Old World. The most familiar is the Hazel or Common Dormouse *Muscardinus avellanarius* of Europe and Asia Minor. This is the Dormouse in *Alice in Wonderland*, which falls asleep at the Mad Hatter's tea party: its name derives from *dorm*, meaning sleep. In Victorian times it was a popular pet in Britain. It is found mainly in deciduous woodlands, often associated with hazels and honeysuckle. It grows to about 14 cm, of which the furry tail is just under half, and weighs about 15 gms, but up to 40 gms just before hibernation. Excellent climbers, Hazel Dormice build globular nests in a dense bush or in the base of a coppiced stump. They usually have 2 litters a year of 3–5 young after a gestation of about 23 days. They are independent at about 7 weeks, and have lived 4 years in the wild and 6 in captivity. When the temperature drops below 16 °C they go into hibernation, and during hibernation their blood temperature can fall as low as .25 °C – its normal temperature is 34–36 °C.

The Garden Dormouse *Eliomys quercinus* is another European species occasionally seen in zoos, but the most frequently exhibited is the Edible or Fat Dormouse *Glis glis* which is widespread in Europe, as far east as the Volga River, and on most of the larger Mediterranean islands. It was also introduced into Britain at the turn of the century. It was eaten by the ancient Romans (hence its name), who fattened them in earthenware pots on acorns, chestnuts and fruits. In some areas, particularly where there are orchards, the Edible Dormouse can be a pest and cause considerable damage, especially to stored fruit. It gives birth to 2–10 young after a gestation of up to 30 days and the young are independent at about 4 weeks. They have lived over 8 years in captivity.

PORCUPINES

Indian Crested Porcupine

North American Porcupine

There are 2 families of porcupines: the 12 species of Old World porcupines and the 9 species of New World porcupines. New World porcupines are mainly arboreal; Old World species mostly terrestrial, burrowing rodents. The Old World porcupines are found throughout Africa and southern Asia, and the Crested Porcupine *Hystrix cristata* occurs in parts of Europe; it is also widespread in Africa as far south as Tanzania and Zaire. The other species of Old World porcupine commonly seen in zoos is the Indian Crested Porcupine *H. indica* which is found throughout the drier parts of the Indian sub-continent. The long quills on the back can be erected into a crest, but contrary to popular belief they cannot be propelled at attackers; they are merely rather loosely attached at the base so that if they become embedded in an attacker they detach themselves. Sceptic wounds from porcupine quills embedded in tigers' paws have been the cause of tigers becoming man-eaters.

The North American Porcupine *Erithizon dorsatum* is found from northern Alaska, across northern Canada and the north-eastern USA and the western States as far south as northern Mexico. It grows to a length of up to 86 cm, plus a tail of up to 30 cm, and weighs up to 7 kg – occasionally much more. The preferred habitat is mixed woodland and forest, but it lives in a wide variety of other habitats from tundra to desert. A single young (occasionally twins) is born after a gestation of up to 217 days and is active soon after birth, reaching maturity at about $2\frac{1}{2}$ years, and has lived for over 10 years.

CAVIES

Wild Cavy *Cavia tschudia*

There are 6 species of Cavy or Guinea Pigs including the Domestic Guinea Pig *Cavia porcellus*. The precise origins of the Domestic Guinea Pig are obscure, but it is known to have been domesticated in South America for at least 3000 years, and it is quite distinct from any living wild relatives. It is primarily bred for meat production and during the Inca Empire (AD 1200–1532) a number of strains were developed with different colour patterns and meat qualities. After the arrival of the Spanish *Conquistadores* some breeds were lost, and the area in which they were kept was reduced. They are now raised mainly in Peru, Bolivia, and Ecuador, where they often run in and around the huts of the native people, in much the same way as chickens in other parts of the world. It has been estimated that over 60 million a year are consumed in Peru alone. The Spaniards brought the Guinea Pig back to Europe (as in the case of 'Guinea' fowl, the English name simply acknowledges it was a foreign animal!) and since that time they have been popular as pets and are bred in several distinctive varieties. They have also become important laboratory animals. After a gestation period which averages 68 days, up to 13 young are born. However, the young in such large litters rarely survive and the normal litter size is 2–4. The young are born well-developed, covered in fur, with eyes open and able to follow the mother soon after birth, and take solid foods as well as milk the day they are born. They develop rapidly and have mated successfully when only 3 weeks old, but are normally sexually mature at about 3 months. They have lived 8 or more years in captivity.

The Rock Cavy or Moco *Kerodon rupestris* is also exhibited in many zoos, and is also easily domesticated and makes good eating.

Domestic guinea pigs

MARA *Dolichotis patagonum*

The Mara or Patagonian Cavy is a rodent looking rather like a deer or hare, that lives in open arid areas of central and southern Argentina. They grow to a length of up to 75 cm plus a tail of 4.5 cm and weigh up to 16 kg. Although related to the Guinea pigs and Cavies they have evolved a body shape more like deer, and on the hind feet 3 toes have rather hoof-like claws. The fore-feet have 4 toes, which have sharp claws that are used in excavating their burrows.

Maras are active by day, spending the night in their burrows. They are extremely fast, and have been timed to run for over 1 km at 45 kph. They walk when moving slowly, but also hop like a rabbit, gallop and start or spronk – jumping on all 4 feet together. They usually live in small groups, but occasionally in herds of up to 40, but they do not have territories with pairs staying together. They breed throughout the year and each female is capable of producing up to 4 litters a year. After a gestation of about 3 months 1–3 young, usually twins, are born in the open. They are active soon after birth and move into the burrows. The young are weaned at about 11 weeks and mature at about 8 months. They have lived up to 14 years in captivity. Maras are very popular exhibits in zoos and there are many flourishing colonies, breeding through many generations.

The closely related Salt Desert Cavy *Dolichotis salinicola*, found in Bolivia, Paraguay and Argentina is smaller than the Mara with a band of yellowish-white from the belly to the base of the tail. In the wild Maras are thought to be declining due to competition with the introduced European Hare.

CAPYBARA *Hydrochoeris hydrochaeris*

The Capybara is the largest living rodent growing to
a length of 1.3 m, standing up to 50 cm at the shoulder
and weighing over 50 kg. It is found from Panama
south, east of the Andes, to Uruguay and northern
Argentina. Capybaras are semi-aquatic, living in
densely vegetated areas close to rivers, lakes and
marshes. They hide in thick vegetation by day and
emerge in the evening and early morning to feed, but
in areas where they are persecuted they have become
nocturnal. When disturbed they run with a galloping
gait and take to the water, where they dive and swim
with only the nostrils, eyes and ears above the surface
– as do the hippos of Africa. They feed on land,
mostly on grasses, but also on aquatic plants and

melons, squashes and other crops. The breeding season varies geographically; gestation periods of up to 156 days have been recorded and the litter size ranges from 1–8, but normally about 5. The young are active shortly after birth, following their mother and eating grass, and they are fully weaned at about 16 weeks. In captivity they have lived over 12 years. The Capybara is of considerable economic importance. Although it is sometimes an agricultural pest, it is also hunted for its valuable hide and fat; in some areas over-hunting has caused it to become rare. However, it is still widespread and in some places it is now being ranched commercially. The Capybaras' main enemies are the Puma and Jaguar, although smaller carnivores may take young animals. In captivity they become very tame, and are often seen in zoos.

PACA

The Paca or Spotted Cavy *Cuniculus paca* and the Mountain or Taczanowski's Paca *C. taczanowskii* are found from Eastern Mexico to Paraguay, and in the Andes of Venezuela, Colombia and Ecuador, respectively; the Paca has been introduced into Cuba. Pacas can grow to a length of nearly 80 cm, plus a tiny tail of 2–3 cm, and weigh up to 10 kg; the Mountain Paca is smaller. Both look like giant Guinea Pigs and live in a wide variety of habitats, but usually near to water in forests; the Mountain Paca occurs between 1800 and 3000 m in the Andean Paramo, the Paca, usually at lower altitudes, but occasionally up to 3000 m. They are nocturnal, living in burrows, among rock-clefts and tree roots, from which they emerge at dusk to

Paca or Spotted Cavy

feed on a wide variety of vegetable matter including seeds, fruit, leaves and shoots. They are rarely social, living singly or in pairs. The female Pacas give birth to 2 litters a year, after a gestation of about 118 days; there is usually a single young, occasionally twins. A Paca has lived over 20 years in captivity; they breed regularly, and have been bred through several generations. In the wild they sometimes do considerable damage to crops. Throughout their range they are hunted, not only because of the damage they cause, but also because their flesh is extremely popular, and often highly priced. Excessive hunting has exterminated them in many areas.

The Pacarana or False Paca *Dinomys branicki* is found in forested montane regions up to 2000 m, from Colombia to Bolivia. It is not particularly closely related to the true Pacas, but superficially looks very like them and has a similar patterning. It grows to a length of up to 80 cm, plus a rather long tail of up to 20 cm, and weighs up to 15 kg. Since its discovery in the late nineteenth century, the Pacarana has never been common. Several times it has been considered extinct and it is thought to be becoming increasingly rare due to overhunting, as with the true Pacas, its meat is very popular. Although they are rather docile animals (despite their name which means 'terrible' or 'thunder' mouse) they do not appear to thrive in captivity and are rather rare in zoos.

BRAZILIAN AGOUTI *Dasyprocta aguti*

There are about 12 species of agouti, found in Central and South America and in the Lesser Antilles. They are large rodents that probably fill the same ecological niche in the New World as the small deer, such as Duikers (p. 340) and Muntjac (p. 278) in the Old World. They run on their toes, which are elongated and hooflike. However, in some ways they are more rat-like; for instance, when feeding they often sit on their haunches and hold their food with their forefeet. They are mostly active by day, feeding mainly on fruit and other vegetable matter, sometimes storing surplus food in holes. Agoutis are the 'basic diet' of many South American predators such as the Jaguar, Coati and Boa Constrictor; they are also a popular item of food with the peoples living in and

around their forest habitat. However, despite heavy predation they are often extremely abundant. They live in forest, thick scrub, savannahs and farmlands. They normally live within easy access of a water supply, and they usually have well-worn tracks and pathways coming from their nesting sites. Agoutis produce a litter of 1–3 young after a gestation of up to 120 days; the young are active and able to run about within an hour of birth. They are weaned at about 20 weeks. Although there is a very high mortality among young agoutis in the wild, once fully grown they can live a long time and in captivity have lived over 17 years. Although some species have suffered from the destruction of their forest habitat, the Brazilian (or Orange-rumped) Agouti seems to thrive in many of the newly made habitats among farmland. They have also been introduced into the Caribbean islands as far north as the Virgin Islands. These introductions were by the native Carib populations, long before the European colonists arrived, and they were there for sufficient time to develop into distinct subspecies. However, with the arrival of Europeans, and the subsequent destruction of the forests, they have declined and some became extinct. Agoutis are popular zoo exhibits; several species are kept, the Brazilian Agouti being the most common and it breeds freely. The closely related Acouchis *Myoprocta* spp are also occasionally seen. There are 2 species, the Green Acouchi, *M. pratti* and the Red Acouchi *M. Acouchy* from northeastern South America.

PLAINS VISCACHA
Lagostomus maximus

The Plains Viscacha is the largest member of the Chinchilla family, growing to a length of up to 66 cm plus a tail of up to 20 cm, and weighing up to 8 kg; males are nearly twice the weight of females. The Plains Viscacha is found in the grasslands of Argentina, and in a small area of southern Paraguay, where they construct elaborate burrows known as *viscacheras*. They may contain up to 30 entrances, extend over 600 m² and have been known to be occupied for several centuries.

Some of the entrances are nearly 1 m deep, and during the building of a tunnel Plains Viscachas may excavate 80 m³. On the mound of earth from their excavations Viscachas often collect a sort of 'museum' of inedible objects gathered from the surrounding countryside, among which may be stones, bones and human refuse. The large burrows of Viscachas provide homes for a number of other animals including snakes, lizards, toads, owls, other rodents and even predators such as Boa Constrictors and Foxes which may feed on the Viscachas. Viscachas live in colonies of up to 50 and in the more northerly warmer parts of their range they have 2 litters a year, in other areas only 1. After a gestation of up to 166 days, 1–4 (usually 2) young are born. They are weaned at 2 months, and mature at anything between 5½ and 15 months. In captivity Viscachas become very tame and they can be seen in a few zoos where they have lived for over 9 years. In the wild they are becoming increasingly rare and although once extremely abundant have now been exterminated from most of their range. The reasons are two-fold: first the large burrows often cause humans and cattle and horses to stumble and break limbs, and its urine has a harmful effect on the soil, secondly, its thick fur is highly valued by the fur industry, and so it has been heavily hunted.

The 3 species of Mountain Viscachas *Lagidium* spp. also have dense soft fur which is highly valued in trade, and have also as a consequence suffered serious declines. However, they are rarely exhibited in zoos.

443

CHINCHILLAS

Long-tailed Chinchilla

There are 2 very closely related Chinchillas: the Long-tailed Chinchilla *Chinchilla laniger* and the Short-tailed Chinchilla *C. brevicaudata*. They grow to about 38 cm plus a tail of up to 15 cm, and weigh up to 800 g; the females are larger than the males. The fashion for making clothing from Chinchilla fur goes back at least until the Incas. Their fur is now among the most valuable in the world, and this is because it is incredibly fine, soft and dense, with up to 60 hairs growing from each follicle. Chinchillas live high in the Andes at altitudes of 3000–5000 m, the Short-tailed Chinchilla was once found at higher altitudes in Peru, Bolivia, Chile and possibly Argentina, but is now confined to Chile, and the Long-tailed Chinchilla is confined to one small area in Chile. Their decline is almost entirely as a result of over-hunting for the fur trade – in the 1900s over 500,000 Chinchilla pelts were exported from Chile each year. Since the 1920s the Long-tailed Chinchilla has been bred in fur farms in very large numbers, and it is this species which is commonly seen in zoos; however, the Short-tailed Chinchilla is the more valuable species. Chinchillas live in barren, rocky areas in rock clefts and burrows, emerging in the evening to feed on leaves, seeds and fruits; occasionally they have been seen to sun-bathe. Chinchillas usually produce 2 litters a year, of up to 6 young, after a gestation of about 111 days. The young are weaned at 6–8 weeks and mature at about 8 months. In captivity they have lived for over 20 years.

Chinchilla sunbathing in the early morning

HUTIAS

Desmarest's Hutia from Cuba
Capromys pilorides

The Hutias are a group of large rodents related to the Coypu (p. 448) confined to the islands of the West Indies. Several species are only known from the remains of their skeletons, and have become extinct since the arrival of man on the islands, and several others are critically endangered. On the island of Hispaniola (Haiti and Dominican Republic) 6 species of Hutia *Plagiodontia* spp have been identified of which only 1, *P. aedium*, survives. It grows to about 40 cm plus a tail of 15 cm and weighs up to 1.2 kg. This Hutia lives in forests and is nocturnal, feeding on fruit, roots and tubers, and also crops. They give birth to 1–2 offspring, after a gestation of up to 150 days, and have lived nearly 12 years in captivity. The remains of the other Hispaniolan Hutias have often been found among the food remains of human settlements, and they probably became extinct before the end of the seventeenth century, due to over-hunting. The sole surviving species is threatened by not only hunting, but also habitat loss and predation by introduced mongooses. A small population of Dominican Hutias has been established in captivity.

The Jamaican or Brown's Hutia, or Indian Coney *Capromys browni* is already extinct on Swan Island, and is rare on Jamaica, but a small captive population appears to be self-sustaining. The greatest diversity of Hutias occurs on the island of Cuba and adjacent islands where there are 8 species, 6 of which are threatened. Like the Hispaniolan Hutia, the main threats to the Cuban species are over-hunting and deforestation. The only other living hutia is found on the Bahamas, *C. ingrahami*. However, several other extinct species are known from Hispaniola, Cuba, Puerto Rico and the Virgin Isles, all of which were probably exterminated as a result of man's activities.

COYPU *Myocastor coypus*

The Coypu is a large rodent, growing up to a length of over 60 cm plus a tail of 40 cm, and weighing up to 10 kg, occasionally more. Looking like a large rat, they are usually the animals displayed as giant sewer rats in circuses and street fairs. Originally found in aquatic habitats in South America from Chile and Argentina to southern Brazil and Bolivia, the Coypu has been extensively introduced into other parts of the world on fur farms. Some of these have escaped and Coypu now live in Europe, Soviet central Asia,

Japan, Canada and the USA. In the 1920s many fur farms were started for their valuable fur (known as Nutria to furriers). However, the market collapsed and they were either released or escaped from poorly built pens. Coypu have subsequently become serious pests in some areas they have colonised. In Louisiana, Coypu trapping has become an important industry and by the 1950s it was estimated that there were 20 million in the wild and in one year near 2 million were trapped. In their native South America they are also utilised for food and occasional attempts have been made to popularise it in Britain; it is apparently illegal to sell it for human consumption in the USA. Coypu are prolific breeders, producing 2 litters a year of 2–9 (usually up to 5) young, after a gestation of 130 days. The young are fully-furred and active, and can be independent a week after birth, but usually remain with the mother for 6–10 weeks, and are sexually mature at 3–7 months. Coypu are popular zoo exhibits and breed freely. They have lived over 6 years in captivity.

Coypu head showing incisors

Coypu burrows in riverbank

PIKAS

American Pika

There are about 14 species of Pika, occurring over most of northern Asia; the Northern Pika *Ochotona alpina* is the only species to occur outside Asia. It is found in Siberia, north-east China, Hokkaido and in North America from Alaska to New Mexico. The American Pika *O. alpina princeps* is found in south-west Canada and western USA, and the Collared Pika *O. alpina collaris* in north-west Canada and

Alaska. They grow to about 20 cm long, and have no external tail and weigh around 200 gms. Pikas have 5 well-separated fingers and toes and are quite unlike rabbits and hares; however, they have teeth very similar to them. Northern Pikas live in mountainous regions, and are one of the characteristic animals of the Rockies. They are active by day and their bleating call can be heard as they scamper away among rocks. Pikas make haystacks in preparation for the winter; they gather grasses, leaves, sedges and other plants and leave them to dry in the sun. During the winter months they remain active, tunnelling beneath the snow and feeding on their supply of hay, which can amount to 6 kgs. However, they do not feed exclusively on hay during the winter, but also forage for roots and grasses. The males and females live separately for most of the year with well-marked territories, but in the spring the male extends his territory to include a female and they defend the territory together. A litter of 3–4 is born after a gestation of 1 month. Their eyes open after about 10 days, and they start eating vegetation 2 days later; they are very active and playful within the nest, which they leave at about 1 month. Pikas usually have 2 litters a year, and they first start breeding the year after their birth. They can live up to 7 years, but few live beyond 5. Although pikas are diurnal and would probably make attractive exhibits in zoos, if sufficient space could be given for their territories, they are comparatively rarely seen, and only a few zoos breed them regularly.

COMMON RABBIT *Orytolagus cumiculus*

The Common Rabbit is the ancestor of all the domesticated breeds of rabbit. It was originally found in Iberia and North Africa. Within historic times man has spread the rabbit over much of Europe, many of the Mediterranean islands, the Azores, Madeira and Canary Islands, and many remote oceanic islands. It was introduced into Chile in the mid eighteenth century, and have spread to Argentina; in 1859 they were introduced into Australia and shortly after into New Zealand, and in both countries have caused hundreds of millions of dollars worth of damage to sheep grazing, crops and have also competed with native animals. The rabbit grows up to 45 cm plus a short, fluffy tail of up to 7 cm, and weighs up to 2.25 kg. They are usually colonial burrowing and forming complex 'warrens'. The burrows are about 15 cm in diameter, and can extend many metres underground. To 'breed like a rabbit' has become to mean a rapid breeding cycle, and in theory they can produce over 30 young a year. The average litter is 5 or 6, born after a gestation of up to 33 days; the young leave the nest when 3 weeks old and are weaned at 4 weeks, when the mother may have started another litter. Rabbits are mainly grazers, feeding on grasses and other flowering plants, but they also eat bark and shoots, particularly in hard weather, and they also cause considerable damage to crops such as winter wheat. Rabbits are preyed on by a wide range of animals, including Stoats, Foxes and Buzzards. In order to reduce rabbit populations the virus disease *Myxomatosis* was introduced into many areas including England, France and Australia; although it initially sent rabbit populations crashing, they soon developed a certain amount of resistance. Domestic breeds of rabbit are important as both meat and fur producers, and also as attractive pets. Many of the latter breeds are kept in zoos, particularly in the 'Childrens' Corner'. Meat breeds reach weights of over 7 kg, and the Rex breeds have short, velvety fur; Angoras have long, soft fur, Belgian hares have a hare-like appearance, the Dutch are small, black and white, while Siamese are white with dark extremities like Siamese cats.

HARES

Brown Hare

Hares are widespread, occurring through the northern hemisphere and Africa. They have also been introduced into South America, Australia and New Zealand. One of the most widespread of all is the Brown Hare, *Lepus capensis* which is found throughout Europe and northern Asia, and over most of Africa, except the forests and deserts. It grows to a length of up to 70 cm has a short tail, and weighs up to 6 kg. They live in a very wide variety of habitats, but are most abundant in open, deciduous woodlands and cultivated lands. Brown Hares do not have a permanent nest but make a shallow scrape known as a 'form'. After a gestation of 42 days 2–4 young (leverets) are born, fully furred and with their eyes

454

open. A day later they can run and a week later are weaned.

The Arctic Hare *L. timidus*, is found across the northern tundra habitats of Europe, Asia and North America, and also in the Alps of Europe. It grows to a length of up to 70 cm plus a short tail of up to 10 cm, and weighs up to 5 kg. The Arctic Hare is white in winter, but most populations moult into a grey-brown pelage in summer. The populations on Ellesmere, Baffin Island and Greenland stay almost pure white even in summer, while those in Ireland never turn white but keep the brownish coloration. Arctic Hares sometimes congregate in herds particularly in the more northerly parts of their range. Wild hares and rabbits are only occasionally exhibited in zoos.

Arctic Hares are important prey items for several species of bird including Golden Eagles

ELEPHANT SHREWS

Chequered Elephant Shrew

The 15 species of elephant shrews are found over most of Africa, except for the west, in a variety of habitats ranging from semi-desert to forests. Although they are insectivorous and shrew-like in many ways, they are often thought to be most closely related to rabbits and rodents; they vary from rat- to mouse-sized.

The Rufous Elephant Shrew *Elephantulus rufescens* grows to 15 cm, plus a tail of 16.5 cm, and weighs up to 50 gm. It occurs in the savannah country of East Africa from Somalia to Tanzania. Like most elephant shrews, it is primarily diurnal, ground-living and hops when disturbed. It lives in pairs in burrows among rocks, in termite mounds and tree roots. One young (occasionally 2) is born after a gestation of 50 days; it is active from birth and independent at 2 months, with a life span of up to 3 years. Elephant shrews are preyed on by many small carnivores, birds of prey and snakes. Their relatively large size and diurnal habits make them better exhibits in zoos than the smaller, more secretive insectivores. Other elephant shrews occasionally exhibited include the Short-eared Elephant Shrew *Macroscelides proboscideus*, from South Africa, and Chequered Elephant Shrew *Rhynchocyon cirnei*.

Rufous Elephant Shrew

Index of English Names

Index of Latin Names

474